Maria Welch Harris, H. D Rumsey

United States Girls Across the Atlantic

Maria Welch Harris, H. D Rumsey

United States Girls Across the Atlantic

ISBN/EAN: 9783744686181

Printed in Europe, USA, Canada, Australia, Japan

Cover: Foto ©ninafisch / pixelio.de

More available books at **www.hansebooks.com**

United States Girls
Across the Atlantic.

THE ANCHOR LINE OF STEAMSHIPS.

BY MARIA WELCH HARRIS.
HOMER N. Y.
1876

H. D. KEARNEY, Photographer
HOMER, N. Y.

TO THE THREE

WHO IN YOUTH DIRECTED THE THREE PARTS OF HER NATURE IN WAYS OF RELIGION, LEARNING AND HEALTH —

TO

H. HARVEY, D. D., Professor at Madison University,
S. B. WOOLWORTH, LL. D., Sec. Board of Regents, Albany,
C. GREEN, Physician at Homer, N. Y.,

THIS BOOK IS MOST RESPECTFULLY DEDICATED BY ONE OF THE THREE UNITED STATES GIRLS,

MARIA WELCH HARRIS.

Truair, Smith & Bruce, Printers and Binders,
"Journal Office," Syracuse, N. Y.
1876.

	PAGE.
THE OCEAN VOYAGE,	9
GLASGOW AND AYR,	16
SCOTTISH LAKES,	20
STIRLING, EDINBURG AND MELROSE,	28
LONDON,	35
PARIS,	52
SWITZERLAND,	69
PASS TETE NOIRE TO MARTIGNY,	83
CASTLE OF CHILLON. LACUSTRINE CITIES.*	
THE AAR AND JUNGFRAU,	87
THE HOME OF TELL,	97
LUCERNE,	101
MUNICH,	111
INNSPRUCK INTO ITALY,	119
VENICE,	126
FLORENCE,	142
NAPLES,*	150
ROME,	168
NORTHERN ITALY,	187
HOMEWARD BOUND,	192

* ILLUSTRATIONS OPPOSITE PAGE 84.—1. Chamois. 2. Castle of Chillon.
ILLUSTRATION.—5. (Opposite page 158,) Mold of Dead Man found at Pompeii.

BREVITY is the soul of wit, and it is also a desirable characteristic in the preface of a book; but the writer can scarcely permit the opportunity to pass without a few words to the friends for whom this volume was prepared. A package of letters is stored away in the secret drawer of one of the Three, kind words are treasured in the storehouse of Memory, and Imagination accompanies these pages to the pleasant homes where teachers, and pupils, and the friends of all days, read and talk of the wanderings of their independent friend. Accept most heartfelt thanks for your prompt replies and generous offers, and be assured that labor has been amply rewarded, as is always the case with the labor of love.

THE OCEAN VOYAGE.

Chapter I.

IT was at the close of spring-time, 1873, that we United States Girls left our homes to become a party of adventurers. We did not call ourselves *triumviri*, for not a man entered our ranks; we were scarcely *triumfeminæ*, for one of our number could not yet claim the name of woman; but we were, nevertheless, three, crossing the broad Atlantic to visit the Old World.

We did not represent many of the professions so actively pursued in Uncle Sam's dominions, for one had not reached the age to choose her walk in life, and one was a lady of leisure; one of the three had for a score of years borne the name of teacher.

We adopted as our watchwords, Independence and Self-Reliance, and, with sachels and shawl-straps, boldly entered upon our journey. We were among the first to go on board the *California*, and we lingered upon the deck to make a survey of our fellow-passengers, who came in such numbers that we feared for the capacity of the ship to harbor them all comfortably; but when the bell sounded as a signal for departure, the crowd went toward the land, and the few remained to embark upon the bosom of the deep. The day was all that human beings could ask, — bright and beautiful, giving promise of future good to both land and sea — of spring-time and harvest to the one, of prosperous voyage and safe return to the other. The people on the shore waved a long adieu, to which the voyagers responded heartily. Slowly but surely we moved away, and soon the connection with those upon land was only by the unseen bonds that unite kindred hearts, however wide they may be separated. Beautiful beyond description was the first day's sail; — calm and peaceful was the deep, and clear and bright was the dome of heaven. The sun sank peacefully behind the waters, and the moon and stars looked familiarly upon us. With a feeling of trust we went to our berths, and we said within our hearts that it was a good beginning.

Equally promising was the following day — the first day of the Summer — and it was also the Sabbath day upon the sea as it was upon the land. The church bell sounded at the usual hour, not, however, from lofty tower, sending its peal through hill and dale, but calling in unmistakable tones to assemble for the worship of God. Closing the eyes to all evidences of the fitness of the room for administering bodily food, we were permitted to receive spiritual food at the hands of a pastor from the sister State of Kentucky. The remainder of the day was not particularly marked in its observance as the one in seven, but was pleasantly spent in friendly intercourse.

The hours thus far had been bright, golden ones, and the vessel seemed a miniature world sent adrift on the ocean of space — sailing on and on to find its orbit far beyond the lesser stars which dotted its course when first it was launched. No excitement disturbed the breast of the passengers save when the report became current that a lady with children had left her well-filled trunks in the hands of a careful husband and they were still safe on dry land. The question was freely discussed how they should manage to procure a change of garments and all the little conveniences of travel. The sachels of the three contributed something to alleviate the perplexities of the occasion. The monotonous round of chit-chat and game, and the measured walk over the deck of the vessel was occasionally varied by the sound of the bell at the regular hours for meals. First of all, at 7 A. M., it invited to partake of the wholesome oatmeal served in various ways — in porridge or gruel, with milk or sugar, and at the table of the dining-room or in the berth of the state-room; at 8:30 to breakfast; 9:30, children's breakfast; 12, lunch; 1, children's dinner; 4, dinner; 6, children's tea; 7, tea; 9 to 11, supper. To these numerous calls the response was ever ready, and the long lines of tables were crowded to the utmost with the one hundred and twenty-five first-class passengers. But on the fourth morning there was a change in the state of affairs, and the teacher was waked at 4 A. M. by the smaller third of their party "calling for New York," as they say on shipboard. Hastening to assist the sick and afflicted, she soon learned that charity begins at home, so she and her charge lay down together, and comforted and consoled each other to the best of their ability. There was no sunshine that day, only clouds and rain and dismal cold weather — thermometer at 35°. But a blessing on the pure air of heaven, how reviving it was, and is, and ever will be, especially to the sea-sick. The deck was almost deserted, except by those on duty, and a few who still had sufficient strength to seek the fresh sea air. A strong arm was offered at the door, and a chair was placed in a spot somewhat sheltered from the rain, and it was held for an hour in spite of wind and storm. No, we retract, the wind blew the chair and its occupant over upon the deck, and a seat in the form of a beam was taken. We must all yield to the elements when in a state of active exercise, especially if they are assisted by life-exhausting nausea, so with all the grace attainable under the circumstances, she descended to the regions below, and they saw her no more that day. We had been sailing in a northerly direction in a line nearly parallel with the shore of our own loved land, and off the banks of Newfoundland we saw the last living creature whose home is not on the bosom of the deep, two of Mother Carey's chickens flying out in quest of food.

We received ample compensation for early rising on Wednesday, the fifth day of the voyage. We hastily responded to the call to come upon deck and see an iceberg, and the remembrance of the sight will be a joy forever. We were five miles off Cape Race, lat. 45 deg. 1 min., long. 51 deg. 56 min. Airy and white, it seemed a creation of fancy, and we scarcely dared turn our eyes for fear that when we looked back again it should have gone from our sight forever. On it sailed, like some monster cathedral raising its lofty spire high toward heaven's gates. The hues were varied as the sunlight fell upon it from different directions (this was about the only glimpse of sunshine we had for seven days), and it assumed a variety of forms as we left it in the distance. Can Strasbourg or Milan equal this creation of nature's architect? This was but one of a number, and soon we were surrounded by icebergs both great and small. One seemed an Esquimaux hut with a smaller one by its side, one a noble fort manned by imaginary heroes, stiff, stern and cold, standing at the post of duty till their life-blood flowed away. In the varying light, dark evergreens rose in the background, and the picture was complete. The largest one was thought to be about two hundred feet above the surface of the water, and half a mile distant from the ship.

Day after day we were only occasionally assured that there was a living being in existence except the four hundred persons on board the steamer *California*, and that by the sight of a far-distant sail. Oh, how broad the Atlantic is! — yet we did not feel ourselves so insignificant as we had supposed we should when upon its bosom, but, on the contrary, as we stood in the centre of the ship she seemed to reach from horizon to horizon, and her masts and sails to take a strong hold upon heaven. We felt that man had been almost enabled to hold the ocean with an iron hand, and to enforce submission by the breath of steam. But the grandeur and the beauty of the ocean, mortal need not attempt to describe, nor pen to paint. Imagination cannot picture it; every moment it changes, every wave is different. The grandest sight was reserved for the last. As we approached the shores of the Old World, and we thought the land would hold out her arms to receive us, the winds and the waves seemed determined to retain us in their power. They rocked us so vigorously that sleep was driven from our eyelids for the first time since we had trusted ourselves to their care. Many made their appearance with anxious looks, to learn the cause of the commotion. The scene was more than beautiful. Once again the sun had made his appearance in the midst of white, fleecy clouds, chasing each other over the bluest sky that the hand of Nature can paint — a real October sky. The waves lifted their foaming crests, then bowed as if in silent adoration, then melted away in flecks of foam and emerald green too lovely to imitate Toward the sun a sheet of silver sheen overspread the whole, and we seemed to be sailing on a sea of glass. Nature never seems complete without a thing of life in her midst; and so the sea-gulls in great numbers gloried in this bright scene, and presented their ebon bodies borne upon white wings. The passengers had been tossed about until they were afraid to move, and placed themselves in some position which they supposed secure; but alas for the fallacy of human hopes! A gentleman who was very gallant in bracing himself to steady a lady, found himself seated upon the floor by her side; one young lady, finding a wave in rather too close proximity to her skirts, to save herself from a wetting, swept books and papers from the lap of her friend and sent them flying in all directions. It was too much to see the labor of hours swept away in a breath, so with a frantic rush she went after them. Backward and forward they rolled, letters, chairs, men, women and water, (only one sheet sailed away on the wings of the wind; did it reach its destination on the American shores?) All of a sudden the sound of the engine was hushed, and the waves rolled higher than ever; the vessel was turned about, like a steed at the will of his rider, and although seeming to resist to the utmost, it was still forced to obey the guiding hand. Now came the solution of the matter; owing to the entire obscuring of the sun's rays for seven days, only dead reckoning could be taken of the ship's course, and when our captain expected to see the green land of Erin, suddenly emerging from a blinding fog, he found himself just off the shore of Tyree island, away to the north of Scotland, and in danger of being dashed in pieces upon her rocky coast; so in haste he gave the order to stop the motion of the vessel, and we were thrown into the trough of the sea and became the plaything of the waves for a time. A day's more sail brought us to Moville, where we put off passengers at the dead of night, under a broad, full moon, which was just appearing in sight.

"Blessings brighten as they take their flight," is a lesson we learn early in life, but we realized on Wednesday, the 11th day of June, that they brighten still more as they come back to sight. There is scarcely any night in this northern latitude at this season of the year, so we had not thought to be up with the morning, but we had hoped to be on deck when our steamer entered the Clyde. Our first sight of "Bonnie Scotland," however, was Ailsa Craig, a mountain of stone rising from the water almost directly in our course. This black rock was first presented to sight as if to bring us back by degrees to our lost estate; then Holy Island rose before us, a rock to be sure, but picturesque in form and having its barenness covered with a velvety green robe of moss. Had we forgotten how the land looked, the green grass of our native soil? or had these far-away coasts borrowed the emerald green of the sea and bedecked themselves for our landing?

Eleven days at sea had made the earth a paradise, and we were in a state of perfect delight. We were introduced to the mountains of Scotland by a sight of Goat Hill, rising also from the water, its base and sides covered with moss and evergreens, and its peak high up among the clouds. Mt. Stuart, home of the Marquis of Bute, the "Lothaire" of Disraeli, and Rothsay Castle, where the Fair Maid of Perth was kept a prisoner, showed us what art can do when combined with nature, and strongly reminded us that we were in the land of Scott, whose song and story have made the world familiar with these interesting localities.

Fairly within the land, the banks upon each side presented a view never to be forgotten; bays, harbors, yachts, light-houses and castles bewildered and almost entranced us. The first British engine gave us a shrill welcome to their shores; handkerchiefs waved a glad greeting, and the pack of hounds on the beautiful lawn wagged their tails with delight. The larks sang the old, old song as they settled in the branches of the trees, which also told the story of age. But the sad story of centuries ago was forcibly brought to mind at sight of Dumbarton Castle. We knew that we must meet at every turn mementoes of the unfortunate Mary, Queen of Scots, whose fate had brought a tear in childhood and many a sigh in later years. This day of sight-seeing was rendered perfect by a view, indistinct though it was, of the friend of old, Ben Lomond. He had his nightcap on, as usual, and the rusts of ages crept slowly over his brow.

All pleasant things must have an end, so it was with our sail up the Clyde. Just before we reached the place of landing we met a steamer bound for the American shores; the hearts of the three went along with her, but their faces looked toward the land of the East, where they hoped to wander under Italian skies and through fields of snow during the days of the coming twelvemonth.

GLASGOW AND AYR.

Chapter II.

THE royal authorities acknowledged the independence of the United Three, and sent them on shore without deigning to notice the sachels and shawl-straps. Immediately begins the search for things new and old. We see at once that the houses stand on a solid foundation, and that there is a great sameness in form and color; not a white house, not a house of wood — all stone or brick, and dingy brown. The people too, stand on a sure foundation — that of honesty; they take the world slow and easy, and are never too much hurried to be courteous and kind. If you ask a question which they do not understand, they "beg your pardon," and if you require a favor they "thank you."

The modes of conveyance looked somewhat strange, the fancy Hansom cabs and the cozy wagonets, drawn each by one noble-looking horse. In but very few instances are seen two horses working side by side; it is either one or three. In one of these wagonets (an open omnibus for four) we went over the city of Glasgow, with one stout Scotch horse. We visited the Cathedral, famous for its antiquity and for its stained glass windows, which are modern, one having been presented by Queen Victoria, which cost six thousand dollars. The Necropolis, one of the most beautiful of cemeteries, stands near the Cathedral, a monument to John Knox crowning the summit of the high hill. Now begin to be repeated the names which were learned in childhood, but which the learner knew not where to locate; for as we rode along the Bromislaw, one of the finest river-side drives in Europe, we were reminded that here once lived two famous Scotch characters, who differ greatly in the reputation which follows them, as they doubtless did in the lives so long past — Rob Roy and Robert Burns. One beautiful feature of this city, which is second only in Scotland, are the crescent parks, smiling and beaming like the new moon on all who come within their sight. People seem to live in the streets, as one might judge by the crowds which fill them. The travelers learned to use the Scotch umbrella, and did not forget it during their stay in Glasgow, for it rained and the sun shone so much together that they became inseparable companions.

From Glasgow it is customary to make many pleasant excursions, and, perhaps, first among the number is that to Ayr, the home of Burns.

> "Auld Ayr, whom ne'er a town surpasses
> For honest men and bonnie lasses."

We could but draw a contrast, standing in the ticket office at the depot in Glasgow. So many minutes before the departure of the train a door was unfastened and the crowd came in single file, passing slowly along, almost as at a funeral. No one jostled his neighbor — no one pressed by to procure his ticket first; altogether it was a new sight, and we said, "Sloo, but sure Scotch."

When we left Glasgow we made our first acquaintance with European cars, an acquaintance which, though continued through the next twelve months, never tempted us to transfer our preferences from the more convenient and agreeable ones of home travel. The coaches all open in the centre and upon both sides, but the doors are not of much service most of the time, for they are closed and fastened before the train starts, and the conductor is only occasionally seen walking past the window and looking in upon us as though we were prisoners who needed watching.

At the station he takes his time for unlocking the door which is on the side of the depot. On almost every train there are three classes of cars, so that those who wish to travel in ease, or who think their family *unapproachable*, almost *royal*, can take the first-class cars; those whose money has been hard-earned and must go a great way can take the third-class cars, if they can be blind to their immediate surroundings and have their conversation with the new scenes in nature through which they are constantly passing. Those that are neither one nor the other can take the middle class, so everybody may be suited.

Through Paisley, whose shawls had not much attraction for us, in a southeasterly direction, toward the coast along which we had sailed when we were leaving the Atlantic and upon which we hoped to cast our farewell glance when we should embark again after a year of wandering, and the home of the poet is reached, the poet who, in his short life of less than thirty-eight years, furnishes the example of a single man who has rendered classical his native tongue by the outpouring of poetry and song. A short survey of the High Street of Ayr, and in the little wagonet we hasten on to scenes more closely connected with the hero of the hour. Two miles through a broad street, which June had made green in oft-returning summer, and which Burns keeps green in the memories of his admirers, we pause before the walls which echoed his first cry, and swift as Time the years of his childhood glided away, and in maturer years we plainly heard him say:

> "To you I sing in simple Scottish lays
> The lowly strains in life's scenes."

ILLUSTRATIONS.—Ayr, the Home of Burns. High Street with the Braes of the River Doon, two miles and a half from Ayr, on the left, and the old Bridge of Doon, which figures so prominently in Tam o' Shanter's flight, on the right. Statues of Tam o' Shanter and Souter Johnnie in a grotto in the Cemetery of the new Church of Alloway. Tam o' Shanter's Inn. New Bridge of Ayr and Old Bridge of Ayr. Burns' Cottage, where the Poet was born, with the Relics of Burns—his Bust and Portrait and the Bible he gave his Highland Mary, on the left, and the Monument of Burns, sixty feet high, raised in 1820, on the right. Robert Burns and Highland Mary with the Banks of Doon (Monument in distance) on the left, and the Old Church of Alloway, scene of the Witches' Dance in the Poem, Tam o' Shanter, on the right.

Univ. of

And we heard him describe the Cotter's Saturday Night, when

> "Wi' joy unfeigned brothers and sisters meet,
> And each for others' welfare kindly spiers;
> The jovial hours, swift-winged, unnoticed fleet;
> Each tells the uncos that he sees or hears.
> The parents, partial, eye their hopeful years,
> Anticipation forward points the view;
> The mother wi' her needle and her shears
> Gars auld claes look amaist as weel's the new;
> The father mixes a' wi' admonition due."

Our hearts beat in sympathy when we remembered the words:

> "From scenes like these old Scotia's grandeur springs,
> That makes her loved at home, revered abroad.
> Princes and lords are but the breath of kings,—
> An honest man 's the noblest work of God!"

Our thoughts ascended in the prayer:

> "O Thou who poured the patriotic tide
> That streamed thro' Wallace's undaunted heart,
> Who dared to nobly stem tyrannic pride,
> Or nobly die, the second glorious part,
> Oh, never, never Scotia's realm desert."

Burns' cottage is now used as a small public house. Half a mile further and again we stood before an old churchyard, and in memory, aided by imagination, went back to the time of Tam o' Shanter, when he had lingered at the old inn with Souter Johnnie, till

> "The time approaches when Tam maun ride.
> That hour, o' night's black arch the key-stane,
> That dreary hour he mounts his beast in.
> Weel mounted on his gray mare Meg,
> A better never lifted leg,
> Tam skelpit on through dust and mire,
> Despising wind and rain and fire;
> Whiles glow'ring round wi' prudent cares,
> Lest bogles catch him unawares,
> Kirk Alloway was drawing nigh,
> Where ghaists and houlets nightly cry.
> * * * Tam saw an unco sight,
> Warlocks and witches in a dance.
> There sat auld Nick in shape o' beast,
> A loosie tyke, black, grim, and large,
> To gie them music was his charge.
> Coffins stood round like open presses,
> That showed the dead in their last dresses,

> Wi' mair so horrible and awfu'
> Which even to name wad be unlawfu'.

"Tam stood like one bewitched," then

> "Laist his reason a'thegether
> And roars out, "Weel done, cutty-sark!"
> And in an instant all was dark;
> And scarcely had he Maggie rallied,
> When out the hellish legion sailied."

Feeling as though the witches were after us, we rode on to the "running stream they dare na' cross," where

> "Nannie, far before the rest,
> Hard upon noble Maggie prest,
> And flew at Tam wi' furious ettle;
> But little wist she Maggie's metal.
> Ae spring brought off her master hale,
> But left behind her ain gray tail."

This was by the Auld Brig o' Doon, and we rode by its braes where the poet said,—

> "Oft hae I roved by bonnie Doon,
> To see the rose and woodbine twine;
> And ilka bird sang o' its luve,
> And fondly sae did I o' mine."

Last of all we visited the monument erected in 1820 to the one whose words are his own best monument. Here are preserved many mementoes of Robert Burns and his Highland Mary, of whom he wrote:

> "The golden hours on angel wings
> Flew o'er me and my dearie;
> For dear to me as light and life
> Was my sweet Highland Mary"

Here is his library and the very Bible he gave to her. All of a sudden, as we went round a projecting corner, there sat Tam o' Shanter,

> "And at his elbow Souter Johnny,
> His ancient, trusty, drouthy crony,"

so natural that we were tempted to flee away, feeling that the witches had not finished their work in this noted town. We left Ayr saying:

> "Read the names that know not death,
> Few nobler ones than Burns' are there,
> And few have worn a greener wreath
> Than that which binds his hair."

A delightful excursion to the Falls of the Clyde, where nature plays most wonderful freaks in rowing her waters to the sea — "a fall of a few feet, a fall of about thirty feet, a cataract of ninety feet, and a grand final leap," — where Romance circles with rainbows of light the dark retreat of the chief of Scottish Chiefs, Sir William Wallace ; and to Lanark, where, in an Established Church of 1777, a colossal statue of this same chief is elevated high over the entrance, as he stands high in their records of fame ; and we leave Glasgow, to return no more till the year again comes around.

SCOTTISH LAKES.

Chapter III.

SCOTLAND acknowledges Rob Roy as one of her most celebrated characters, and everywhere we were met by reminders of this bold mountaineer as we passed through the regions where

> "The eagle he was lord above, and Rob was lord below."

The journey was fraught with interest for its historical associations, and also because

> "It was so wondrous wild, the whole sight seemed
> The scenery of some fairy dream."

Under very favorable circumstances for this country, we took a steamer at the foot of Loch Lomond. No fog or glaring sunlight interfered with our view, and beautiful fleecy clouds sailed in the blue above and were mirrored in the blue below. All around us rose

> "The mountains that like giants stand
> To sentinel enchanted land."

As we glided along on the bosom of this lovely lake, the most beautiful dissolving views were presented, and before we could fairly take in one it became another, each more pleasing than all the rest.

> "The rocky summits, split and rent,
> Formed turret, dome, or battlement,
> Or seemed fantastically set
> With cupola or minaret."

The ghost of Rob Roy seemed to haunt the entire scene, and the dark heather and the broom on the mountain sides to be evil spirits seeking whom they might devour. Many of the Bens "heaved high their forehead bare" in apparent veneration for their hoary brother, Ben Lomond, whose aged head is much of the time covered with the white cap which served as a signal to get ready the Scotch umbrellas. We were constantly shut in by those many mountains, all run in a different mold, some lifting a huge bare peak all unadorned, others bearing vegetation to their very summits, while their sides were varied with the dark moss growing in large patches here and there, intermingled with the broom, which gives great variety by its different appearance at different stages of growth — bright green when young, and becoming very dark, and covered in time of blossoming with the yellow papilionaceous flowers. The numberless little islands were all bowers where Cupid might dwell, and the names of many of them very appropriately commence with Inch, giving only an exaggerated idea of their baby size. Seventeen of the twenty-one miles where this romantic lake finds for itself a bed, winding around at the base of these heathery mountains, receiving to its bosom the leaping, sparkling waterfalls, taking up the burns hastening on their way to the sea, and giving frequent glimpses of realms little less than fairy through the glens and dingles on its sides, — seventeen miles among the islands Inchcruachan, Inchgalbraith, Inchtaranach, and all the other Inches, from the wee ones with scarcely soil for a single tree to find root, to Inchlonaig, where are still growing the yew trees planted by Robert Bruce, and Inchmurrin, the largest of Lomond's isles, measuring a mile and a half in length by three-quarters of a mile in breadth, where one of Scotland's dukes now feeds his deer, — seventeen miles the U. S. G. sailed from the foot of the lake, where the Leven takes these waters on to the Clyde, to within four miles of its head where it receives Falloch Water. We landed at Inversnaid in the face of two tall Bens across the lake, and in the neighborhood of Craigroyston Cave, where Rob Roy oft retreated to hold council with his men. At Inversnaid a fort was built in 1715 to overawe the Macgregors, with Rob Roy at their head, which was commanded by General Wolfe; but now the peaceful Inversnaid House invites the traveler to roam at will through these romantic regions, and to rest in safety within its walls, without fearing to hear the sound of the slogan or to catch a glimpse of the Highland robber. The next morning our omnibus was filled with twenty-two persons, and, drawn by four horses, we rode up the mountain sides in the midst of heather and blue bells, and saw the long-haired cattle and sheep feeding where the foot of man could scarcely tread; the little lambs, with black feet and noses, frisked and played as only lambs can do; past the house (a small part of which remains) where Helen Macgregor, the wife of Rob Roy, was born; by the side of Inversnaid burn, which throws itself down to Loch Lomond in a fall of thirty feet; up and on beyond wee lochs and tarns, five miles from Loch Lomond to Loch Katrine and the lines of Wordsworth to the Highland girl at Inversnaid found a ready response:

> "Now thanks to Heaven, that of its grace
> Hath led me to this lovely place;
> Joy have I had, and going hence,
> I bear away my recompense.
> In spots like these it is we prize
> Our memory, feel that she hath eyes."

The ride was ended at Stronachlachar, where,

> "One burnished sheet of living gold,
> Loch Katrine lay beneath us rolled,
> In all her length far winding lay,
> With promontory, creek and bay,
> And islands that, empurpled bright,
> Floated amid the livelier light."

Soon we stood on the deck of the dainty little steamer *Rob Roy*, and were in the Lady of the Lake country, where all the incidents of that beautiful poem seemed to be re-enacted. We sailed amid "islands that, empurpled bright, floated amid the livelier light," and as we approached Ellen's Isle, where

> "The wild-rose, eglantine and broom
> Wasted around their rich perfume,
> The birch trees wept in fragrant balm,
> The aspens slept beneath the calm,
> The silver light, with quivering glance,
> Played on the water's still expanse."

We heard the hunter wind his horn,

> "When lo! forth starting at the sound,
> From underneath an aged oak
> That slanted from the islet rock,
> A damsel guider of its way,
> A little skiff shot to the bay
> That round the promontory steep
> Led its deep line in graceful sweep."
>
> "The boat had touched this silver strand
> Just as the Hunter left his stand
> And stood concealed amid the brake
> To view the Lady of the Lake.
> The maiden paused as if again
> She thought to catch the distant strain,
> With head upraised and look intent,
> And eye and ear attentive bent,
> And locks flung back and lips apart,
> Like monument of Grecian art,
> In listening mood she seemed to stand,
> The guardian Naiad of the strand."
>
> "A chieftain's daughter seemed the maid;
> Her satin snood, her silken plaid,
> Her golden brooch, such birth betrayed."
>
> "And never brooch the folds combined
> Above a heart more good and kind.
> Her kindness and her worth to spy,
> You need but gaze on Ellen's eye."
>
> "Impatient of the silent horn,
> Now on the gale her voice was borne:
> 'Father!' she cried; the rocks around
> Loved to prolong the gentle sound.
> Awhile she paused, no answer came;
> 'Malcolm, was thine the blast?' The name
> Less resolutely uttered fell,
> The echoes could not catch the swell.
> 'A stranger, I,' the Huntsman said,
> Advancing from the laurel shade.
> The maid, alarmed, with hasty oar
> Pushed her light shallop from the shore,

> And when a space was gained between,
> Closer she drew her bosom's screen."
> * * * "Though fluttered and amazed,
> She paused and on the stranger gazed."
> "On his bold visage middle age
> Had slightly pressed its signet sage."
> "His limbs were cast in manly mould,
> For hardy sports or contests bold."
> "Slighting the petty need he showed,
> He told of his benighted road."
> "A while the maid the stranger eyed,
> And, reassured, at length replied,
> That Highland halls were open still
> To wildered wanderers of the hill."
> "The stranger viewed the shore around;
> 'Twas all so close with copsewood bound,
> Nor track nor pathway might declare
> That human foot frequented there,
> Until the mountain maiden showed
> A clambering, unsuspected road,
> That winded through the tangled screen
> And opened on a narrow green,
> Where weeping birch and willow round
> With their long fibres swept the ground.
> Here for retreat in dangerous hour
> Some chief had framed a rustic bower."

We had not time to visit this bower and with the hunter spend the night where "the stranger's bed was of mountain heather spread," but we seemed to hear him name his rank:

> "The Knight of Snowdoun, James Fitz-James,
> Lord of a barren heritage,"

and to hear him say:

> "This morning with Lord Moray's train
> He chased a stalwart stag in vain,
> Outstripped his comrades, missed the deer,
> Lost his good steed and wandered here."

We imagined we saw, on the morrow,

> "The parting lingerer wave adieu,
> And stop and turn to wave anew."
> "While yet he loitered on the spot,
> It seemed as Ellen marked him not,
> But when he turned him to the glade,
> One courteous parting sign she made."

ILLUSTRATIONS.—1. Ellen's Isle, on Loch Katrine. 2. The Trosachs.

Univ.

Eight lovely miles amid these beauties were passed as a song, the entire length of this miniature lake, and we reached the enchanted land.

> "High on the south huge Benvenue
> Down on the lake in masses threw
> Crags, knolls and mounds confusedly hurled,
> The fragments of an earlier world;
> A wildering forest feathered o'er
> His ruined sides and summit hoar,
> While on the north, through middle air,
> Ben-an heaved high his forehead bare."

We did not enter the Trosachs, as in the days of the Lady of the Lake, by a ladder composed of the branches and roots of trees, nor, like James Fitz-James, guided by the rebel chieftain, Roderick Dhu, but like him we went through "a profound defile, a craggy gorge, a dark crevasse, wild, wooded, beautiful and sublime."

> "All in the Trosachs glen was still,
> Noontide was sleeping on the hill."

And where King James the Fifth of Scotland (for it was no humbler character than he who was the hero of Scott's poem) looked upon his own brave steed, in imagination we heard him say:

> "Ah, gallant grey,
> For thee, for me, perchance 'twere well
> We ne'er had seen the Trosach's dell."

Pause ye who will with James Fitz-James and Roderick Dhu at Coilantangle ford, where

> "Each at once his falchion drew,
> Each on the ground his scabbard threw,
> Each looked to sun, and stream, and plain,
> As what they ne'er might see again,
> Then foot and point and eye opposed,
> In dubious strife they darkly closed."

We left them to finish the fight, and our poetic journey through the Scottish lakes being ended,

> "Soon the bulwark of the North,
> Grey Stirling, with her towers and town,
> Upon our fleet career looked down."

STIRLING, EDINBURG AND MELROSE.

Chapter IV.

STIRLING — home of many of the sovereigns of Scotland, scene of many of the disasters of the most unfortunate family of Stuart, city which was long capital of Scotland, and which still contains buildings raised by four of the Jameses — stands on the right bank of the river Forth, thirty-six miles from Edinburg. It commands a point of that river which was long the main passage between the Highlands and Lowlands, and it is second to no place in Scotland except Edinburg.

Stirling is a place of interest for many reasons, and we immediately sought the Castle upon its wedge-shaped hill, ascending three-quarters of a mile to an altitude of two hundred and twenty feet, and stooping precipitously to the northwest. Imagine the exquisite beauty of the panorama spread out before us. In the distance, the Grampians, the Ochil Hills, Tinto, and Arthur's Seat thirty-six miles away; just at its base, the linked Forth winding itself in graceful curves which are often so deep that it nearly unites with its own waters. Then count the battle-fields where the fate of nations has been decided — fourteen, bearing bloody records. The history of Scotland's chief, Sir William Wallace, comes plainly to mind. When John Baliol, great-grandson of David by his eldest daughter, and Robert Bruce, grandson of the same by his second daughter, contended for the throne; and when Baliol had placed himself and his country under the power of Edward I. of England, who had sent a governor to lord it over the Scots, the patriotic heart of Wallace could not submit, and he slew the son of the governor, and was an outlaw for five years, living in the forests and caves of his native land. Then, with an army, he held the castle of Stirling, and fought, in 1297, the famous battle which still bears the name of this castle, and which a colossal statue of Wallace commemorates. It was here that he gave his characteristic reply to those demanding surrender: "We came to assert our rights, and to set Scotland free." Would that we could leave him here in the midst of his glory, but history will not allow it ; so we follow him through nearly ten more years of varied victory and defeat, and find him a prisoner in London Tower, and see him die, only thirty-seven years of age, not, as the romance says, of a broken heart, but dragged to Smithfield, beheaded, and his body quartered and placed in the four extremes of the realm, as a warning to those who dared resist the claims of England. But the world will always mourn that so brave a patriot met so cruel a fate.

Another of the battle-fields, and the last we have time to mention, is Bannockburn. Three miles from the height where we now stand, the guide points out a flagstaff rising from the *Bore Stane* where Bruce planted his standard, in 1314, when he addressed his army with the words :

> " Scots, wha hae wi' Wallace bled,
> Scots wham Bruce has often led,
> Welcome to your gory bed,
>   Or to glorious victory ! "

Some received one and some the other, for it was then and there that the independence of Scotland was gained and Bruce was seated on the throne which his descendants held for so many years. This castle was sometimes called the Castle of Snowdoun, hence James V., whom we have followed in his romantic and almost fatal visit to the Lady of the

Lake, was called the Knight of Snowdoun; and we visited the room where

> "Motionless and moanless drew
> His parting breath, stout Roderick Dhu,"

who had been wounded in the encounter with James at Coilantangle ford, and in a sort of dream, in which the closing incidents of Scott's immortal poem were enacted with life-like distinctness, we took the cars for Edinburg.

With minds crowded with these scenes of greatest historic interest, we reached the end of our journey.

> "Edina high in heaven wan,
> Towered, templed, metropolitan,
> Waited upon by hills,
> River, and wide-spread ocean."

It was ten o'clock in the evening, scarcely past the twilight hour in that northern latitude, and we walked to our hotel with eyes sharpened by Imagination, and we looked upon the old, old city painted with the brush of Fancy. We rested one day, and on Monday morning commenced the examination of Edinburgh, daughter of that fortress of rock which has been a stronghold from the days of the Saxon heptarchy, now a city more than seven miles in circuit, containing two hundred thousand inhabitants. From whatever standpoint we could take, Edinburg Castle stood out in bold relief, hence we immediately directed our steps toward this mountain supposed to have been occupied by forts from times before the Christian era. The castle crowns the summit of Greenstone rock, 445 feet high and 700 yards in circumference. The entrance is over a drawbridge, across a deep, dry fosse, through a gateway, up a causeway, through an archway, etc., etc.; in short, an enemy would be obliged to pass through nine gates (if gates were there, and they could easily be replaced if necessary,) in face of shot and shell, to gain the highest point, the King's Bastion. We pause in our ascent before the "Old Royal Palace," the abode of the kings and queens of Scotland. The

VIEW OF EDINBURGH

FIRTH OF FORTH

FROM THE CASTLE

room of Queen Mary is shown, where James VI. was born. He was let down from the window in a basket and sent to Stirling to be christened. This room is nine feet long, very irregular in shape, and would be uninteresting were it not for the associations connected with it. A gentlemanly Highland officer conducted some of our party into the sergeants' mess-room and showed us the portrait of their beloved Queen, lately received. He also pointed out the Time Gun, which is discharged every lawful day at one o'clock by means of an electric apparatus attached to the Nelson monument on Calton Hill, a mile away.

We have reached the summit of the castle, are on the King's Bastion, and before us is Mons Meg, the hero of army cannon, crippled to be sure, but giving unmistakable evidence of having been in many battles. Forged in 1476, used in the seige of Dumbarton Castle in 1489, burst in 1682, removed to London Tower in 1754, it was restored to Scotland, mainly through the intercession of Sir Walter Scott, in 1829. It is thirteen feet long and weighs more than five tons. It stands sentinel on the highest point of the castle, just in front of St. Margaret's Chapel. This chapel is the oldest building in Edinburg and the smallest and most ancient chapel in Great Britain. David I., the founder of this chapel, was also the founder of Holyrood Abbey, and it was during his reign that the city was first raised to the rank of a burgh, in 1129.

We left Castle Hill to thread the Canongate, made famous by the "Chronicles" of Scott. It derives its name from the Augustine canons of Holyrood. The Canongate is Scottish history fossilized. What

---

ILLUSTRATIONS.—1. Edinburg from the Frith of Forth — Arthur's Seat, Salisbury Crags, Calton Hill, Castle. 2. Edinburg from Castle Hill, Mons Meg in the foreground; Scott's Monument on Prince's street at the left; Calton Hill, with its monuments to Dugald Stewart and Nelson, the National Monument to the Scotchmen who fell in the battles of Napoleon, and the new Royal Observatory. Holyrood Palace, at the foot of Calton Hill, just back of the bridge. St. Giles' Church, on High street (its square tower surmounted with an imperial crown), of which John Knox was pastor at the Reformation, where Jenny Geddes threw her stool at the Dean of Edinburg, and where the Solemn League and Covenant was sworn to and subscribed in 1643. Grayfriars' Churchyard, where many of the Covenanters are interred.

ghosts of kings and queens walk there! What strifes of steel-clad nobles! What wretches borne along, in the sight of peopled windows, to the grim embrace of the "maiden!" What lamentations over disastrous battle days! James rode up this street on his way to Flodden. Jenny Geddes threw her stool at the priest in the church yonder. John Knox came up here to his house after his interview with Mary at Holyrood — grim and stern and unmelted by the tears of a queen. In later days the Pretender rode down the Canongate, his eyes dazzled by the glitter of his father's crown. Down here of an evening rode Dr. Johnson and Boswell, and turned into the White Horse Close. David Hume had his dwelling in this street, and trod its pavements, much meditating the wars of the Roses and the Parliament. One day a burly ploughman from Ayrshire, with swarthy features and wonderful black eyes, came down here and turned into yonder churchyard to stand, with cloudy lids and forehead reverently bared, beside the grave of poor Ferguson. Down the street, too, often limped a little boy, Walter Scott by name, destined in after years to write its "Chronicles." Later still came those philanthropists and Christians, Chalmers and Guthrie, gathering abundant material for their "ragged schools." And last of all came the United States Girls from across the Atlantic, on their way to Holyrood, — "*Monasterium Sancta Crucis de Crag*," Monastery of the Holy Rood (or Cross) of the Craig.

The cause of the erection of the abbey was this: The king had gone hunting on the day on which was commemorated the Exaltation of the Cross. He followed a stag, which stood at bay, and would have injured him, but a piece of the true cross slipped into his hands. He was warned by a vision "to big an abbey of Channones Regular in the same place quhare he gat the crace." Hence the Abbey of Holyrood was founded by David I. in 1128. Now it is roofless and falling to ruin, and the remorseless rain falls on the graves of David II., James II., James V.

and Lord Darnley, the husband of Queen Mary. A palace rose long ago by the side of the abbey and in connection with it, and the principal events in its history are in relation to Mary, Queen of Scots. On the second floor were her apartments, and there her bed still stands, surrounded by hangings of crimson damask, with green silk fringes and tassels, and tapestry illustrating the fall of Phaeton. It looks as though it would fall to pieces if the hand but touched it, so plainly is age written thereon. Just outside the door to descend by a back passage is the blood of Rizzio, which is as ineffaceable from the floor as is the story of his tragical death from the minds of those who learned it in childhood.

We have but just begun to tell of the castle, the palace, and of this strange city, but it has been so beautifully described by poets, philosophers, and divines, that we only dare to say we have walked these old streets, looked upon these old walls, visited the home of John Knox, read the inscriptions upon the walls of his house, entered the church where his voice sounded so fearlessly, and stood by the stone in the pavement which, by the initials "J. K.," marks his resting-place. We have been in the churchyard where the martyrs repose, and have seen the "Maiden" (too cruel for such a name) which severed their heads. We have counted the stories of the old houses till we came within one of a dozen, and we have ascended the steps between the old and the new town till our limbs refused to move. We have walked over Calton Hill, conspicuous for its monuments, and spent three hours climbing that we might sit upon Arthur's Seat and there date letters to send to our friends in America (we feared that the wind would serve us worse than it did upon the ocean if we attempted to do more than to date our letters, so we took a lower seat to write them); and we rejoice to have stood by the monument reared by Scotland to the son who has brought such honor to his country, Sir Walter Scott.

We bade good-bye to Edinburg with sad hearts. We would not believe that we should come no more into her streets, hear the pleasant greeting of old and young, and look upon the honest faces of those Highland Scotch people. No! let us rather believe that we shall some time live over again those pleasant days, even though it be an illusion. Nine days were spent in this city, so often compared to ancient Athens crowned with her Acropolis, and one day in the suburbs at Hawthornden, eleven miles away — classic Hawthornden, where the poet Drummond resided and received his friend Ben Jonson (who walked from London to visit him) under the noble sycamore tree which still spreads its branches to shelter the weary traveler — through the picturesque glen on the bank of the North Esk river, which can scarcely be surpassed in Scotland, a mile in length and containing about twenty species of wild flowers, and also some curious caves, one of which was occupied by Bruce for four years; then we left for Melrose, not quite forty miles from Edinburg. We waited "to view fair Melrose aright, and visit it by the pale moonlight," so the afternoon hours were spent in a walk to Abbotsford, three miles on the banks of the Tweed. Abbotsford, the residence of Sir Walter Scott, "a romance in stone and lime," embodies portions of Melrose Abbey, Holyrood Palace, Linlithgow Palace, and Edinburg's old Tolbooth, so arranged as to make it a grand museum. "It is beautiful in itself, beautiful in its surroundings, and beautiful in the memory which it perpetuates." Within was the library with its twenty thousand volumes; the study, where the author of "Waverley" prepared those works which took the world by storm, and which has been left very nearly as he occupied it; the armory, which has the ring and clang of steel in the air; and the drawing-room, in which Sir Walter died, with its old furniture of ebony, its beautiful carvings and stained-glass windows. A few of the very interesting objects in this place were: Queen Mary's seal and snuff-box, Rob Roy's purse, Bruce's candlestick, key of the old Tolbooth, and the bust of Scott after death. We were obliged to leave his great-granddaughter, twenty years of age, in peaceful possession of these collections of art and antiquity, and walk again over the ground his feet had trod so many times, with the bracing air from Scotland's hills and the bright sun from Scotland's skies coming down upon us, back to Melrose. Having returned to the neighborhood of that grand old ruin, which the poet tells us to view by pale moonlight, we are so anxious to get a glimpse within the mural enclosure that we set forth before the sun has left the sky, thinking to surround the walls of the noble abbey and steal a glance at the hidden relic. We recall to mind that it was the work of the same David who reared Holyrood and gave to Edinburg her fortress on Castle Hill — three splendid creations destined to stand the test of time and to be a wonder to coming generations centuries after the one who designed the whole had passed away. Melrose was a suitable monument to Robert Bruce, who gave to Scotland the independence since lost, and a fit mausoleum, too, for his patriotic heart, which had been prepared by his countrymen to be taken to the Holy Land, while his body was laid to rest in a neighboring abbey. With hearts burning with enthusiastic patriotism, the earth was hardly the place for our feet, and we had climbed as high as was possible under the circumstances. The three had scaled a lofty stone wall, not questioning whether it was laid by Picts or Scots, or whether by the Romans seeking a new world to conquer. All in file we stood, like soldiers surveying a battle-field after the fight is finished. Fearing to take too much from the pleasure of the evening, one kind sister descended from her high position and extended a hand to those still above. The teacher first accepted the proffered hand, and with one bold leap confidently expected to land on terra firma. But problems in algebra could be more readily solved, French comedies more politely played, German verbs more musically inflected, or cantos in Virgil more gracefully rendered; for all of a sudden there was a whirl of the brain, a holding back by strong power, an entire suspension of movement, then a sudden giving away, a crash and a fall, followed by a cry that the little one had carelessly jumped upon her friend. Opening her eyes to the condition of things, she saw with wonder the *American Coon* (an epithet applied to the smallest one of our party by a facetious friend, in allusion to her name) perched above the fallen of the party, looking sympathizingly from her elevation, while coldly extended before her eyes lay the barefaced perpetrator of the deed, holding her fastened to the ground. A huge stone had caught her skirts and held her suspended for a time in mid-air, then yielding the point, had followed her and still held her captive as with heavy chains. After a careful examination to see whether a fracture or a sprain or only a bruise was the result of the accident above mentioned, the three concluded to return to the hotel as speedily as possible; so, with an arm on the shoulder of each of her companions, she hopped on one foot, and the landlady was summoned, the shoe removed, the foot bathed, and our view of Melrose Abbey was *all* "moonshine." The state of affairs next morning was not as bad as had been feared, and taking a broomless handle which offered itself for a crutch, we limped to the depot and left Melrose.

For reasons we need not specify, we did not walk around the English lakes and visit the homes of the poets so celebrated, but we hastened to London, where we knew the halt and the maimed and the lame are wont to assemble. Once on the way, when it was necessary to change cars, a kind-hearted Scotchman saw our condition and invited the crippled one to sit on his truck and be wheeled with our baggage through the long depot — an offer too good to be rejected.

LONDON.

Chapter V.

WE could almost tell when we crossed into England, and bonnie Scotland being left, we held our breaths in suspense as we approached the largest city in the world. We looked upon the green fields separated by hedges of hawthorn, and suddenly we were in the midst of darkness, which was dissipated only by a feeble lamp burning over our heads, lighted we knew not when or how. After a ride of several miles in this way, the cars stopped in the midst of daylight, and they said we were in London. London! Is it possible? Where is the rush, and the din, and the turmoil? where are the beggars, and paupers, and disgusting specimens of mankind? where is the filth, and squalor, and abject poverty? Perhaps we shall see them when we become better acquainted.

The British metropolis in its largest sense is nearly one hundred miles in circumference. It comprises $688\frac{3}{4}$ square miles, and the number of dwellings is estimated at half a million. If placed in a straight line they would extend from the north end of Great Britain to the shores of the Mediterranean. A total length of its streets is 2,500 miles — one-third of the earth's diameter; if stretched in one long line they would reach from Liverpool to New York. The number of streets, lanes and parks in the whole Metropolitan Police District is 10,500 miles. The population is over three and a half millions. All the vehicles travel in the course of a year about as far as the earth is from the sun. "London is no longer a city, it is a province covered with houses." It was in this city that we were set out of the cars to find a home, and we easily found one, for everywhere we saw posted, "Rooms to let," and in a few hours we had taken one, and were ready to see London. Our home in this vast city was not many miles at most from its centre. To the curious we would say that it was on Devonshire street, north of the Thames, and west of St. Paul's Cathedral, which is about the centre of London.

The Thames goes through London from west to east very much as a huge serpent makes its way through tall grass, writhing and coiling and running almost out of sight until you are right upon it. One continuous great thoroughfare runs also from west to east in a more nearly direct course than the Thames, but it takes a variety of names in its different parts, beginning at the west — Uxbridge road, extending along the side of Kensington Gardens and Hyde Park, which lie side by side; Oxford street, New Oxford street, High Holborn (the one which we were nearest), Holborn Hill, Newgate, Cheapside (nearest to St. Paul's), Poultry (nearest the Thames), Cornhill, Leadenhall, Whitechapel, Whitechapel road, Bow road, and Stratford road. Our first attempt at sight-seeing was in a stroll through the three parks, St. James, Green and Hyde, which extend each an angle into the other so as to form one continuous park, terminated by Kensington Gardens, at the extreme western part of the city, which we have mentioned. These parks, as might be expected, surround the homes of royalty. First of all, in Kensington Gardens, two and a half miles in circumference, is Kensington Palace, the birthplace of Queen Victoria in 1809. This is still a royal palace, although not inhabited by royalty. Hyde Park contains 390 acres. At the point where Hyde Park and Green Park overlap each other, at the entrance from Piccadilly, stands a colossal bronze statue of Achilles, cast from cannon taken at the battle of Waterloo, weighing thirty tons, "erected to the Duke of Wellington and his companions in arms by their countrymen." Green Park contains sixty acres, so named probably for its undulating grassy surface. Near where Green Park becomes St. James is Buckingham Palace, which is too small for the family of the present sovereign, but is nevertheless occasionally occupied by her Majesty. Just north of St. James Park, and lying between the Mall and Pall Mall (so named from the old game, *Paille Maille*, a forerunner of croquet,) are two more palaces — St. James, built by Henry VIII., and Marlborough House, where live the Prince and Princess of Wales, who may change their residence some day for one more regal. St. James Park contains ninety-six acres and is considered one of the greatest ornaments to the metropolis.

There is one place in London in which children are much interested, and we sought the spot where the American Coon informed us the Laughing Jackass could be found, according to her little reader. We had not many miles to go, in a northwesterly direction, before we found Regent's Park, a nearly circular enclosure of about 470 acres, in the northern part of which are the famous Zoological Gardens, established during the present century. We sought in vain for the jackass, but found almost every other kind of animal under the sun. The Sloth Bear was a curious specimen of the Bruin family, that acted somewhat like a Sloth, crawling slowly off after the crumbs thrown to him, and back again as slowly, then, putting all four of his paws through the bars of his cage, he would seat himself on his haunches and wait patiently for something else. The kangaroos were numerous, and one was specially interesting with her big baby hopping in and out from her pouch, which was not large enough to hold the whole of it, but allowed its limbs to touch the ground in her frequent turnings after food. We sat down just in front of the cage where the king of the forest was lazily shutting his sleepy eyes; but what was our surprise when he suddenly opened his monstrous jaws and gave a roar that was truly the roar of the lion, and we as suddenly withdrew from his presence. It would be difficult to imagine any form under the sun that was not in Regent's Park that day, and although we walked back in the midst of the rain, we were amply paid for every step we had taken.

We must in truth say that the parks of the city of London do not compare very favorably with the parks of our own country — with Lafayette Park in St. Louis, Lincoln Park in Chicago, Fairmount Park in Philadelphia, and Central Park in New York. Although parts of them are highly ornamented, yet they are not one continued scene of beauty like the ones mentioned. As we walked slowly along we were passed by many ladies on horseback, attended by their servants at a respectful distance. Soon the question as to their destination was solved. We approached a scene of gaiety and excitement — Rotten Row; a street you might call it, in the midst of the park, where assemble daily at certain hours the equestrians of the city. Such a display of fashion and rank and style one seldom sees. The horses here, and everywhere in the country, are noble specimens and pleasant to look upon, and the little boys of ten or twelve years, and the ladies of all ages, (both classes of persons in high hats,) made the scene a novel one.

We were sufficiently fortunate on our approach to Buckingham Palace to obtain a view of the Shah of Persia, with his suite, and the royal family, on their way to a garden party with the Princess of Wales. We could not feel quite the enthusiasm manifested by many of the crowd, because we acknowledge no king or queen, but are our own princes and rulers.

In returning to our London home from a visit to the parks first mentioned, we could pass through Trafalgar Square, whose tallest statue is that of Nelson, high above "Landseer's four noble lions couchant," and the one which has the most curious history is that of Charles the First.

It was made during the reign of the latter king, but when civil war broke out it was sold to a brasier, who was ordered to destroy it. He, however, buried it, and it remained under ground till after the Restoration, when it was erected, in 1674. There is an open space near Trafalgar Square of which we often read, and which is called Charing Cross, from the old village of Charing, where Edward the First erected a cross to the memory of his queen, Eleanor. Wherever her bier rested he erected a cross.

> "A royal game of Fox and Geese
> To play for such a loss;
> Wherever she put down her orts,
> There he—set up a cross."

Thence we proceeded through the Strand, so called because it lies along the bank of the river — in the seventeenth century it was a kind of country road connecting the city with Westminster; under the famous Temple Bar, which is a wide central archway with a smaller one on each side for foot-passengers, the whole dividing the Strand from Fleet street. There are doors in the main avenue, which used to be closed, but are never so now except in case of some state ceremonial, when the royal family knock for admission and the Lord Mayor opens unto them. This is the place where the heads of criminals were exposed after having been boiled in pitch to preserve them. The last ones, those of two Jacobites, were well preserved, for they remained from 1745 till 1772, when they were blown down in a gale of wind. A little way on Fleet street, which has been called the "March of Intellect," it is so full of newspaper and printing offices, then we turned off at Chancery lane, through Red Lion, and so to Devonshire street, ready to rest after the first day in London.

On Tuesday, the first day of July, we visited the Tower of London, the chief fortress of the monarchs of Great Britain and the depository of the national arms and accoutrements. It does not, like its sister

---

ILLUSTRATIONS.—1. Temple Bar. 2. Houses of Parliament. 3. Westminster Abbey. 4. Wesley. 5. Spurgeon.

castles, occupy an elevated position overlooking the surrounding country, but threading busy streets we look with interest upon this structure, which has been palace, fortress and dungeon, in several cases, to the same individual. We have the authority of Shakspeare for saying that the Tower was begun by the Roman conqueror, Cæsar, but most writers date its origin to the time of William the Conqueror, 1078. It is surrounded by a double line of walls and bulwarks, the outer one inclosing thirteen acres. The moat is supplied with water from the Thames, but it has been kept drained since 1846. We enter the walls, fortified by six towers, following one of the wardens dressed in the livery established by Henry VIII. These wardens are often called "beef-eaters," a corruption of *beaufetiers*, battle-ax guards, first raised by Henry VII. in 1485. Within the inner walls, fortified by twelve towers, is the White Tower, a quadrangular structure, erected for William the Conqueror; it has three stories above ground, and, the guard told us, three stories below. Its walls are fifteen feet thick. One division of the first floor is occupied by "Queen Elizabeth's Armory," in which the virgin queen may be seen mounted on a carved horse, attended by her pages and officers of the household in armor. Instruments of torture are shown here, and we saw the thumb-screw applied, very gently, however, to one of our friends. The beheading block and ax were there, used for the last time after the rebellion in Scotland. The Horse Armory is a modern building, in which are arranged equestrian statues of the kings in ancient armor (or "tin pants," our little one said,) from the time of Henry VI., 1422, to that of James II., 1685.

We must not stop to tell of the Bloody Tower, where the two sons of Edward IV. were smothered, or the Bell Tower, where it is said Elizabeth tasted the pleasures of confinement for a time; the Devereux Tower, which derived its name from Robert Devereux, Earl of Essex, the favorite of Queen Elizabeth; or the remaining nine towers, all of which have an interesting history.

It would be pleasant to notice the records of the Tower as a palace, were they not so soon changed to those of a prison in many instances. Henry VIII. gave to all his wives receptions of great magnificence within these walls, but what followed? All was bright to Queen Anne Boleyn in 1533, but in 1536 she inhabited the same apartments, and soon was on her way to the scaffold on Tower Green! — the spot pointed out to us where many had surrendered their lives. History tells of the Tower as a prison.

During the eight centuries the walls of the Tower have frowned upon the Thames, it has not been attacked by a foreign enemy, but during the internal wars which have so often disturbed the country, it has been an object of great importance for each party to gain possession of this impregnable fortress, and therefore it has many times felt the shock of war.

The New Palace of Westminster, or, in other words, the Houses of Parliament, built in consequence of the burning of the old Houses of Parliament in 1834, lies just across the street from Westminster Abbey, extending along the banks of the Thames for nine hundred feet. A royal palace has occupied the same site since the time of Edward the Confessor, who delayed his death, it is said, as long as possible in order to dedicate his abbey. This is probably the finest Gothic structure in the world; it covers nearly eight acres and contains two miles of passages and corridors and five hundred rooms. It is surmounted by numberless towers, but the most important ones are the Victoria Tower, the largest and highest square tower in the world (it bears a flagstaff four hundred feet above the ground, which floats a royal standard twelve yards long and nine yards wide, when the sovereign is within the walls), the Clock Tower, supporting a clock with the largest dial in the world, and the Central Tower, which also has something the largest in the world, but we cannot describe it. Of the five hundred rooms we can notice but few. The House of Lords is ninety feet long, forty-five wide, and forty-five high, and in one part of it is the throne where stands Her Majesty's state chair, approached by three steps; on one side of this stands one for the Prince of Wales, and on the other one for the late Prince Consort, each reached by two steps. The monograms in the compartments of the throne, "V. R.," "P. A.," and "P. W.," show by whom the chairs were designed to be occupied; and the various carvings of roses and *fleurs de lis*, lions and unicorns, shields and escutcheons, tell the history of England for the last century at least. The state chair is somewhat similar to the coronation chair at Westminster Abbey. The House of Commons, too, is no common place after all; but, interesting as it is, we must leave the New Palace of Westminster

Then Westminster Abbey,

> "Where royal heads receive the sacred gold;
> It gives them crowns, and does their ashes keep;
> There made like gods, like mortals there they sleep."

We look back into the ages for the history of this far-famed cathedral, and find that as early as 616 a Benedictine monastery and church were founded by Sebert, King of Essex, on a peninsula formed by the Thames and a small tributary stream, and called Thorney Island, because overgrown with reeds and thorns. It was called the West Minster in reference to its situation with regard to St. Paul's. This church was destroyed by the Danes, and Thorney Island would have passed out of history had it not been for Edward the Confessor, who laid the foundations of the future celebrated abbey in 1065, and caused it to be dedicated eight days before his death. William the Conqueror was crowned here with great pomp in 1065. Little, however, of the work of Edward the Confessor exists in the present building except the foundations, but his name has been perpetuated by one of his successors on the English throne, Henry III., who erected a chapel to his memory, and the bones of the canonized Confessor now rest by the side of Henry III. in the chapel which bears his name. The last great addition to this beautiful structure was the

Temple Bar.

Houses of Parliament.

Westminster Abbey.

chapel of Henry VII., in 1503. The two towers at the western entrance have since been added under the direction of Christopher Wren.

The general plan of the building is that of a Latin cross; length, 416 feet; breadth at the transept, 203 feet; at the nave, 102 feet; height of the west towers, 225 feet. We can hardly tell about the Choir, the Nave, the North and South Transepts, the Chapter House and Cloisters. The interior of the Abbey is grand "with all its mystical effects of light and shade, its lofty arches, its soaring roofs, its glorious windows, and its elaborate sculpture." The building is divided into two tiers of arches of unequal height; above these are pointed windows with different kinds of arches, then a gallery with carved moldings, and still above, lofty windows. Everywhere, on the floor and on the walls, are monuments to the celebrated dead whose dust reposes here. The mosaic pavements in different parts, and the stained-glass windows representing scriptural subjects, add to the beauty and interest of the whole. It is well worth the English sixpence to visit the nine chapels of different dates and listen to the accounts of their builders and occupants, only two of which chapels we will notice. First, Edward the Confessor's, previously mentioned, containing the tomb of this founder of the Abbey, and also the coronation chairs, one of which covers the famous stone of Scone on which the Scottish kings were crowned until 1297, when it was brought to England by Edward I. But grandest of all is the chapel of Henry the Seventh, in the centre of which are the recumbent effigies of Henry and his queen, with hands uplifted to heaven, and surrounded by many devices relating to the union of the red and the white roses. Here too lie Mary and Elizabeth, nearer than they came to each other in their lives, and Cromwell once had a resting-place here, but the royalists took up his body and buried it, decapitated, under Tyburn gallows. Leaving the remainder of the ninety monuments and shrines to royalty, this "acre sown with royal seed," we turn to the Poet's Corner, where, Washington

Irving says, "a kinder feeling takes the place of that cold curiosity with which we gaze on the splendid monuments of the great and the heroic." Oliver Goldsmith gave it the name, and the first monument erected there was to Geoffrey Chaucer, "morning star of English poetry." On one of the tablets we read, "O rare Ben Jonson," and learn that he was buried beneath in an upright position. Many are far removed from this Corner, where their names are read by the curious, as is true of Butler, Gray, Milton and Shakspeare. The monument to Goldsmith contains the line, "He touched no kind of writing which he did not adorn." John Gay wrote his own epitaph :

> "Life is a jest, and all things show it;
> I thought it once but now I know it."

The names of sixty-six — not all poets, however — are indelibly written upon these walls, as their works have impressed themselves upon the world.

Service within its walls gave a new train of thought — a church and a sepulchre combined; fame and a monument afforded by the same tablet; the coronation chair, giving the highest power to a human being, and the bed of death whence all power departs, in close proximity. We visited the chapels, stood before the different carvings upon the walls, admired the stained-glass windows, which alone excel those of Glasgow Cathedral, previously described, and we felt that the day was well spent.

An amusing incident occurred on the morning of the 4th of July. While we three were still enjoying our beds in our new English home, there was a sudden burst, as of fire-crackers, near our walls. Two of our party hastily lifted their heads, with patriotism beaming upon the face and the exclamation bursting from their lips, "It is the Fourth of July!" But they as suddenly disappeared at the suggestion of the Teacher — "Fourth of July in England!"

In this city of a thousand churches, where should we attend divine service? At the Tabernacle, of course, and hear Mr. Spurgeon; and the recollection of the day, and the people, and the church, and the pastor, will remain long with us. Unostentatious but heartfelt were all the services, and six thousand people went to their homes happier, judging by personal experience. His text, "As is the apple tree among the trees of the wood, so is my beloved among the sons of men," led him into a home field, and in apparent sympathy with every heart he delivered a plain, forcible sermon. Standing just below the two galleries, crowded to the utmost, the large choir just beneath him, he took the lead in every exercise, and we wondered how he could have remaining strength to enter the sabbath-school and again conduct the services. May his influence be powerful to raise up others like unto him!

St. Paul's Cathedral, the East Minster of olden times, stands on Ludgate Hill, about the centre of London, and is the most prominent object in the metropolis. It is sufficiently near the truth, guide-books tell us, to say that it is 365 feet high, and there are two handsome bell-towers 222 feet high. Its bell is tolled only on occasion of a death in the royal family. It was built under the direction of Sir Christopher Wren, one architect and one master-mason having been employed on it for thirty-five years, and cost a million and a half of money — a great sum in the seventeenth century, the time when it was built to supply the place of one destroyed by the great fire. We went up to the Whispering Gallery, at the bottom of the inner dome, and seated ourselves to hear somebody whisper from the other side of the dome. Looking straight ahead to the point from which we expected the sound to proceed, suddenly our little girl jumped, turned her head, and asked who whispered in her ear. She examined the wall to find the place whence the sound issued, and insisted that somebody was behind there, and at first we were childish enough to think the same thing, forgetting that we were in the

Whispering Gallery. In the crypt beneath are the tombs of many of England's noble men, and among the number is that of the architect of fifty of London's noblest churches, Sir Christopher Wren ; also of Sir Joshua Reynolds, the painters West and Turner, and of those who fought her battles and gained her victories, side by side, Wellington and Nelson. The outside coffin of the latter was originally intended for Henry VIII. and cost $4,000,000, the proceeds of a tax on coal, the inner one was made from the mainmast of the ship *L'Orient*, captured by Nelson. We ended our visit to St. Paul's Cathedral by a choral service at 3 P. M., when we listened to the grand tones of the organ, and the entire service chanted by the choir.

There was one place in London where we could see the persons of celebrity not merely of modern times but of preceding ages and distant lands. It was at Madame Tussaud's wax-works. There were — as natural as life, we suppose — Henry VIII. and his six wives, all blooming and fresh and beautiful, not looking as though they were going to be beheaded, or divorced, or, what was worse, live with the old tyrant till his days could be dragged out ; the present royal family, and the mother of that same family undergoing the act of coronation before she had even a husband — so contradictory is life ; Shakspeare, and Napoleon III., and our own countrymen too, Washington, and Lincoln, and William Penn, and Tom Thumb ; but not one United States woman. What an interesting day was that spent with characters we had never expected to meet !

All people have their ideas of fairy-land, and ours were fully realized when we visited the Crystal Palace. We do not expect to see anything more beautiful in our life-time, if we reach the allotted age of man. Nature and Art have here combined their powers, and the result is an exquisite production. We were seven hours walking through the building, stopping often, of course, to admire, and once to partake of what became ambrosia and nectar to us, from their connection with so much beauty. We seemed to be in the four quarters of the globe. In the Greek Court we saw the Temple of Jupiter, more than two thousand years old, surrounded by beautiful specimens of Greek art, the celebrated Niobe group, the Venus de Medici, and many others. In the Roman Court the walls were colored in imitation of porphyry and malachite. Venus, Apollo, and Diana, with others of equal beauty, rendered the scene attractive. These were followed by other ancient courts, and these again by the medieval courts of different countries; not the statues, carvings and paintings themselves, of course, but imitations so perfect that one at least who had never looked upon the originals might almost think he stood before them. All these were interspersed with plants and fountains, birds of beautiful plumage, and shells and fishes in their native element; also by the productions of hand and brain to delight the eye and ear. Altogether it was enchanting.

We could hardly be expected to tell all that we saw, describe all that we visited, in this city of cities during the three weeks we were there in '73 and the nine days in '74; but friends may be sure we often went through Threadneedle street and called upon our bankers, J. S. Morgan & Co.; went over most of the fourteen bridges which cross the Thames, and once went under it through the Thames Tunnel; to Bunhill Fields, the "Campo Santo" of Dissenters, and visited the tomb of John Bunyan, where the Pilgrim is represented as making but very little Progress (except in crumbling away) on his monument of stone; and just across the way to the church where Wesley preached his last; to Smithfield, where now is an extensive market, but where once the good and noble were sacrificed; to Guildhall, the Hotel de Ville (Town Hall) of London; around the outside walls of Newgate Prison; steamed under London for many miles by the Underground Railway; saw rough men drink and fight, then walk bootless with the police; had the hat of one of our company shaken by the hand of a shameless woman; and our experience in London was nearly finished. It only remained to visit Victoria in her home at Windsor.

Twenty-two miles in a westerly direction and we approached the residence of her Royal Highness; we saw the walls of the castle at a distance, but no friendly flag threw its colors to the breeze to welcome the three daughters of independent America. We soon learned the cause of this apparent neglect. The Queen had remained longer than is her wont in her winter home at Windsor to entertain the Shah of Persia, and when he left for Paris, she immediately started for her summer residence in Scotland, and so we were unwelcomed. But Windsor is no insignificant place — 10,000 inhabitants — and there was much to be seen if the Queen was not there; her hundred horses were in their royal stables, except the few she had taken to bonnie Scotland, and there were grand views to be seen of the rooms in the palace. Said palace was undergoing a thorough cleaning after its Persian visitation, hence was not open to visitors, even if they did come from across the Atlantic. We went into St. George's Chapel and saw the resting-place of grim Henry VIII., and we wondered how he could rest with but one of his six beautiful wives by his side — Lady Jane Seymour. At the summit of the famous Round Tower of the castle we were amply repaid for our trip by the view of the surrounding country; for miles and miles around it was all one grand park, including several rural villages with all their attractive quiet and comfort, the white spires of their churches pointing heavenward and the white marbles of their churchyards telling that the occupants have departed. In the distance lay the churchyard where Gray wrote his Elegy, sitting, perhaps,

"Beneath those rugged elms, that yew tree's shade,
Where heaves the turf in many a mouldering heap."

When we left the town which provides England's sovereign with a home, we stopped by the way at Eton College, founded by Henry VI. in

1440; at Twickenham, where Pope lived and was buried; and at the Kew Gardens, where the palms are such a wonder to the world, rising to the height of sixty feet in their beautiful crystal home.

One more night within this capital city, and early morning saw us on our way to Dover. We left the shores of "Merrie England," but we entered the limits of a merrier country. We sailed timorously over the restless Channel, known to fathom men's stomachs — not souls; but we anchored safely across from the white cliffs of Dover, took up the sachels and shawl-straps, and spoke the new tongue with all the grace attainable. As the spirits of Rob Roy and Mary Queen of Scots had seemed to make their presence felt in the land of the north we have described unto you, so, in this more southern clime, the eighteen Louises and all the Napoleons have seemed to hover about us.

The transportation from the largest city in the world (at least in this part of the globe) to its nearest rival was quickly accomplished, and the sun which rose upon us in the precincts of the one, shed his parting rays within the walls of the other. Almost all persons tell a story of long delays and troublesome examinations as they pass from one country to another, but the "United Three" walked through their gates undelayed by custom-house officers or officials of any description. All remember the thanksgiving, "Blessed be nothing," and ours is like unto it (sometimes.)

PARIS.

Chapter VI.

FIND friends, we opened our eyes upon this charming city at the witching hour of gas-light, and drove through the mazes of the Champs Elysées until we almost thought we were truly in Elysian Fields. Boulevards, avenues, palaces, statues, fountains, arches, columns, and domes — where are they mingled so beautifully save in fairy-land? Where do they sip the nectar and taste the ambrosia under the open air of heaven, save among those who feel not the needs of the body nor are oppressed by the cares of the mind? Where do flowers bloom and fountains play under the wheels of the chariot and the hoofs of the steed, save in the realms where Beauty reigns and the Beast is a myth? Where does Cupid rule with a golden rod, save in the regions where discord is not? But we will not decide until the morning dawns, and we walk the streets under the clear light of day.

Four weeks a Parisian. What of the city? We have taken observations from the highest points, looking forward from the Arc de Triomphe to the palace and garden famous in the history of this city, the Tuileries; noting the lines of trees that lift their heads toward the Pavilions in that abode of kings and rulers; viewing with wonder Cleopatra's Needle, which adorns the Place de la Concorde, on the spot where the blood of thousands flowed in the troublous times gone by; admiring the com-

Avenue des Champs Elysées, rond-point

PLACE DE LA CONCORDE

bination of nature and art in the flowers of the field and the productions of man in the Champs Elysées; then we have turned backward to the same broad street stretching on to the finest park in the world — the Bois de Boulogne — observing the whirl of carriages and the tramp of feet, the fashion and display, and the marks of need. These two boulevards, with ten others like unto them, meet around this arch, rightly named Arc de l'Etoile, (Arch of the Star,) the rays of which terminate before they reach it, leaving it alone in its glory, bright and beautiful. Nearly every one of the twelve boulevards ends in the distance with some prominent building. This Arch of Triumph was commenced in 1806 by Napoleon I. to commemorate his victories in the East. The four arches are 90 feet high in the centre; the total height is 152 feet, and it is 137 feet square — a grand cube with a passage through its base from east to west and another from north to south. There are four magnificent bas-reliefs of colossal height, and on the vaulting of the great arch are the names of one hundred victories and four hundred generals of the Empire and Republic. But Napoleon the Great was not allowed to do all the carving upon this monument of which Paris is so justly proud. Passing over the reign of Charles X., it was completed by Louis Philippe in 1836. At the close of the late Franco-German war, it must have been a grand sight to see the noblest citizens of France surround their loved arch and stand before the victorious William of Prussia, with arms folded upon their breasts, telling the conqueror that if he rode through it would be over their lifeless bodies. The noble king could afford to pass around, for it was all within his victorious possession.

Walking from the Arc de Triomphe eastward toward the palace of the Tuileries it is one gradual descent half the way and the same ascent the

---

ILLUSTRATIONS.—1. Arch of Triumph. 2. Round Point on the street called Champs Elysees, midway between the Arch of Triumph and the open square. 3. Place de la Concorde.

other half, the first mile and a quarter through the Champs Elysées, then through the Place de la Concorde and the Garden of the Tuileries. These Champs Elysées, fields truly Elysian, were originally a great space covered with prairies and thick gardens, which Marie de Medici began to transform in 1616 by setting out three rows of trees for her own pleasure and that of her court. These alleys still bear the name of Cours de la Reine. Just half way between the Arc de Triomphe and the Place de la Concorde we come upon the Rond Point, (round point,) where are six of the most beautiful fountains constantly throwing off their water in the form of spray and making one feel almost as if walking in the clouds where the rays of sunlight linger and tinge with rainbow hues. Here our boulevard widens and expands and multiplies itself until it is nearly as broad as it is long, ornamented and divided by trees, charming cafés and restaurants, resounding with music, furnishing every sort of entertainment to every age and class. The younger one of our party rode in a petit cabriolet drawn by four milk-white goats, while we occupied the yellow iron chairs and enjoyed the scene. Magnificent flower-beds, called riband-beds, added beauty and variety. It was in the midst of these glorious Fields that the English army encamped in 1815, commanded by the Duke of Wellington, and on the same spot now rises the Palais de l'Industrie, built in 1855 for the great Exposition, but now used for exhibitions of paintings. Passing out from the Champs Elysées between the Horses of Marly, we are in the place which the world knows of under different names at different times. It has been baptized with blood and truly named Place de la Revolution. **At the marriage of Louis XVI. and Marie Antoinette, twelve hundred people were killed** on this spot in the midst of a panic which arose among the people and horses; and later in the lives of this unfortunate pair, blood flowed freely indeed, and they with 2,800 people moistened the earth with their blood in the space of two years and four months. In the centre of this grand Place, where Louis XVI. was beheaded, now rises the Egyptian obelisk, brought at great expense from Luxor, and occupying three years in its transportation. It formerly stood in front of the Temple of Thebes, erected by the great Sesostris 1500 years B. C. It is of rose-colored granite, eighty feet high, and covered with hieroglyphics, not very intelligible, but very interesting nevertheless. On each side of this obelisk is a beautiful fountain, (one devoted to maritime, the other to fluvial navigation,) where eight dolphins spout streams of water on the images in the centre, which falls back to be thrown again. Around the outer part of the Place are eight very large marble statues, which represent the principal cities of France — Lyons and Marseilles, Bordeaux and Nantes, Rouen and Brest, Lille and Strasbourg, (they have the image of the last, if not the reality.) The ground is covered with white sand, and in the sun is glaring and hot, presenting a most perfect contrast to the avenue on the west and the garden on the east, both a forest of trees, and to the magnificent buildings, the Madeleine on the north and the Corps Legislatif on the south across the Seine. In 1814 the Allies encamped here; in 1848 the insurrection commenced here; the constitution of the Republic was read here! What next?

The Jardin des Tuileries (Garden of the Tuileries) was so called because it was a large spot of ground taken by Catharine de Medici, in 1554, as a suitable place to rear for herself a palace which should surpass in magnificence all that had been raised in earlier times. It is about half a mile long, a fifth of a mile wide, and contains seventy-five acres, lying along the bank of the Seine, planted with horse-chestnut and lime trees and ornamented with statuary. Having passed through the garden, where we lingered by the way to listen to the band which plays there nearly every day of the year, we come face to face with what was once the Palace of the Tuileries, and we stand aghast as in imagination we follow old Father Time through the work of three centuries, and in the destruction locks grow gray, his scythe pierces to the very heart, and palaces rise and fall. Here first was the bare brickyard which supplied Paris for four centuries with material for building (*tuile*, hence the name Tuileries,) the spot which Catharine de Medici selected as a site for her palace. We quote from the French: "The labor commenced under the direction of Philibert de Lorme; he had scarcely finished the pavilion of the centre, known now under the name of Pavillon de l' Horloge, and the two adjacent wings, when he was stopped by the superstition of his mistress. An astrologer had predicted that St. Germain would be fatal to her, and, St. Germain being the name of the parish in which her palace was situated, she withdrew to the Hotel of Soissons. She did not escape her fate, however, for the priest who assisted her in her last moments was Lawrence of St. Germain." So we see that the central pavilion, which so long bore the clock of the Tuileries, (just three miles away from the famous Arch of Triumph, hidden there by more than two centuries of time,) was the first of this stupendous building, which has since stretched itself in both directions until it measures about a fifth of a mile in length. At the two extremes of the present royal structure, covering and enclosing sixty acres of ground, the Tuileries and the Louvre were originally located, but Father Time has wielded a wand more than a scythe, and pavilion after pavilion has sprung from the earth and taken its stand by previous constructions, until now it is lengthened beauty long drawn out, and the Tuileries and the Louvre are all one. How many Louises and Henries and finally Napoleons has Time brought into his ranks to act their parts in the drama of life, and fight the battles which are still unfinished — to rear this proud pyramid of man's greatness, and with it fall to the ground in man's weakness; for with Napoleon III. fell the palace of the Tuileries, torn down by the Commune, so that no emperor or king should have a place for his royal head.

We stood in the room of the Louvre where the cruel Catharine, wickedest of women, (who had fled in superstition from the palace to the fortress,) looked across to the bell in the church of St. Germain de l'Auxerrois and gave the signal to begin the massacre of St. Bartholomew — a massacre in which seventy thousand Protestants were butchered, when "the streets were red with blood and the river choked with mutilated bodies." Thence we passed slowly through the almost numberless rooms and the sixteen museums, furnished with the *chefs d'œuvre* of deceased artists and the curiosities and wonders of every age; through the various *salles* — Salle des Caryatides, from the four colossal caryatides of Jean Goujon, who ceased not in his work during the terrible massacre and was shot at his post, (here is the famous Venus de Milo, most magnificent specimen of Grecian art); Salle des Sept Cheminees, in which died the loved Henry IV., first of the race of Bourbon and the one who granted the famous Edict of Nantes — died by the assassin's hand; Salon Carré, containing the richest of gems, Murillo's Conception; Long Gallery, of five compartments, with eighteen hundred of the finest specimens the world furnishes, one devoted to Rubens' pictures; Musée Grec et Romain, the most interesting room, perhaps, in the Louvre, where we see the sceptre of Charlemagne, a shoe worn by Marie Antoinette, and the chair of King Dagobert, who, in the twelfth century, had a hunting-tower on this spot of ground, destined to become so interesting to future generations; Salle de l' Empereur, containing the sword of the First Consul, Napoleon the Great, and the hat he wore in the campaign of 1815, when he came back and took possession of his loved palace — for a very brief period, however; and the Musée des Dessins, where fourteen rooms were filled with models of interesting localities and things — the *Belle Poule*, (the vessel which brought the remains of Napoleon from St. Helena,) the country around Luxor, the home of the obelisk in the Place de la Concorde, etc.

From the Old Louvre, 404 feet square, surrounding the square Court

of the Louvre, through the New Louvre, most modern part of these
buildings, planned by Napoleon I. but finished by Napoleon III. in 1857,
and surrounding Place Napoleon III., we come upon the Place du Carrousel with its Arc de Carrousel, raised by Napoleon I. in 1806 to the
glory of the French armies, and standing just back of what was once
the Palace of the Tuileries. Under this Arc de Carrousel rode, in the
great Exposition time, Napoleon, Alexander of Russia, Bismarck, and
William of Prussia, by the side of Eugenie, under the horses of St. Mark,
(which have since that time been restored to their true owners and we
shall meet them at Venice.) But where is the palace we have come so
far to see — the palace which figured so largely in the French Revolution, to which Louis XVI. came smiling in 1789, but from which he stole
by night in 1792, when his faithful Swiss guards were nearly all massacred — the palace which Louis Philippe entered with the insurgents in
1830, but from which he fled before them in 1848 — the palace which
the nephew of the great Napoleon took under the title of President
of the French Republic, held under that of Emperor Napoleon III., but
was forced to give up with his sword at Sedan ? Where is the Palace
of the Tuileries? We saw everywhere pictures of a burning palace ; we
heard tales of a mad mob clambering up the steps of the imperial
entrance, entering the sleeping apartments of the Emperor and Empress,
drawing caricatures upon the walls, and writing over the doors, " The
French Republic is again declared," and " Liberté, Egalité et Fraternité"; and we saw a long line of ruins facing the beautiful Garden of the
Tuileries and the Arc de Triomphe three miles away. Has old Father
Time, surfeited with reaping, yet laid down his scythe?

Again, from the pinnacle of the Tour St. Jacques we have looked
around upon the many ecclesiastical edifices of the city. Notre Dame,

---

ILLUSTRATIONS.—1. Palace of the Tuileries and the Louvre. 2. Tour St. Jacques (Tower of
St. James.) 3. Church of the Invalides. 4. Cathedral of Notre Dame. 5. Tomb of Napoleon.

UNIV. OF
CALIFORNIA

dating from the sixth century, (or at least from the twelfth,) rich in decorations of art and interesting in historical associations; the scene of nearly every extreme in the life of man; the preaching of the Gospel, offering eternal life unto all who believe, and the taking away of the life of the body; the coronation of the emperor and the baptism of the laborer's child; a hay loft, a wine store, and a church. The Madelaine, designed by Napoleon as a temple of glory, the doors of which church are next in size to those of St. Peter's. The Pantheon, built to receive the ashes of great men — the place where Mirabeau, Voltaire and Rousseau were buried. Sainte Chapelle, a lovely little gothic shrine, constructed to contain the holy relics brought from Jerusalem, but now in Notre Dame. St. Germain de l'Auxerrois, just opposite the palace of the Louvre, bearing the bell which gave the signal for the destruction of the Protestants in the cruel days of Catharine de Medici. The Invalides, rising high above every surrounding object, and marking in colors of gold the resting-place of the great Napoleon. St. Jacques has given us the opportunity of looking down upon these and many other churches; and we have also examined them from a different stand-point, walking their aisles alone and with the busy throng, admiring their beauties and striving to be charitable toward their defects.

"Few buildings in Paris offer greater attraction for strangers than the magnificent monument which is so closely connected with the memory of the first Napoleon. From the reign of Henry IV. an asylum for disabled soldiers was established in an old convent in the Faubourg St. Marcel. Louis XIII. removed it to Bicetre. In order to receive the increasing number of soldiers put out of service by his annual campaigns, Louis XIV. ordered the construction of an edifice, and laid the first stone in 1670. The principal body of this building was finished by Bruant in 1706. It was he who finished the first church. The second, more magnificent than the other, and which is known under the name of the Church of the Invalides, is the one whose colossal dome, 323 feet in height, covers the tomb of the hero of Austerlitz. It is the work of Mansard, and was finished in 1706. The buildings as a whole cover an extent of twenty-eight acres. In 1789 it was called the Temple of Humanity, and under Napoleon, who enlarged and adorned it, it was called the Temple of Mars. Its present name was given to it in 1815. The façade is 612 feet; it is four stories in height, and is ornamented with a profusion of military subjects, bronze statues of vanquished nations, and an equestrian statue of Louis XIV. The galleries which surround the Court of Honor are adorned with paintings of the four historical epochs of France — those of Charlemagne, St. Louis, Louis XIV. and Napoleon I. Provisions are made for six thousand private soldiers a day, three thousand pounds of meat being cooked daily. War is everywhere glorified. Of the sombre reflections which it inspires one sees nothing, except when he regards the mutilated bodies of the occupants of this magnificent edifice." We have translated from a book purchased in sight of this building, but it does not tell the whole story. Directly beneath the dome of the Invalides lies the body of him who said, "I desire that my ashes may repose on the banks of the Seine, in the midst of the French people, whom I have ever loved." Surely mortal ambition ought to be satisfied to rest beneath such a splendid monument. Unwittingly perhaps, Napoleon prepared it for himself; for when informed that his people had become uneasy during his long absence in the wars, he ordered them to gild the dome of the Invalides, and so give the people employment and something new to think about. So the gilded dome of the Invalides towers above everything else, and marks the spot where the Emperor lies. The rays of the sun come through the windows of stained glass, shedding a halo of glory upon everything, down into the crypt where stands his mausoleum, twelve by six feet, on a base of green granite. The pavement is decorated with a crown of laurels in mosaic, and the principal victories of Napoleon are represented by twelve colossal statues of red granite.

Just back of this beautiful church, and seen through the windows between them, is the other church of St. Louis — where military mass is attended every Sunday at 12 — ornamented with the tattered flags of vanquished foes. It was one of the most interesting exercises which we attended, to listen to the martial music and see the files of soldiers march in with measured tread, and the Hotel des Invalides has a prominent place on memory's page.

Where are the ruins of Paris? Where are the marks of devastation and war? Where the sounds of lamentation and woe that reached to our shores but two short twelvemonths ago? Paris in ruins, her people in grief? There *are* marks of the destroyer's hand; there *are* some shattered walls in the midst of surrounding beauty, some buildings razed to the ground; but the work of reparation goes on, and soon the city will be renewed, and perhaps be all the brighter for the cleansing it has received. The Arches of Triumph rise just as proudly in her midst if a few of the topmost stones have been displaced, and the French stand before them with arms upon the breast, bidding the conquerer go around or walk over their bodies. (King William of Prussia was generous enough to do the former.) The Arc de Carrousel, although in the very midst of ruins, stands a memento of former rejoicing — rejoicing when crowned heads rode in gilded carriages beneath this arch, as the fabled goddess still drives her brazen steeds on the spot where stood the famous horses of St. Mark, crowning this arch of joy. And where are the crowned heads? They, too, lie low. Will they rise again, to wear a more brilliant crown? Will the regal hand be stretched forth to resume the sceptre again? Echo answers — Again. The Place Vendome has lost its ornament, the square is without its glory — the statue of Napoleon. First there was the statue of Louis, then of General Bonaparte with the familiar three-cornered cocked-hat, and afterwards the Emperor Napoleon in citizen's dress, which the enraged Commune tore down with ropes when they took the government in their hands. Time will tell whom the French will raise on pedestals in the days to come.

This people have often been censured because they have no word for home in their language. Perhaps they do not need one; they make their streets so attractive, their public buildings so pleasant, their tables in the open boulevards and at the doors of the restaurants and cafés so tempting, the society of one another so desirable, that home may be of minor importance. Certain it is that they seem very happy at their *dejeuners* at noon and their *diners* at six. We cannot vouch for their suppers toward the hour of midnight, as we were never present at this meal. Everybody, from the baby up, drinks wine, but there is certainly less disturbance in the streets, fewer marks of the effect of strong drink, than we see in our quiet little towns at home. The independent three have been great cause of wonder to those who supplied them at the table because they drank what they pleased.

The French must be a domestic people, as their love for pets would conclusively show; scarcely a person walks the street without a quadruped of some kind either in the arms or at the heels. What must have been the state of things before the thirty thousand canines fell victims to cruel war! Speaking of the domestic qualities of this people reminds us of their bread. The first time we sat at a French table we thought the polite waiter had been extremely remiss in placing a stick of wood on one end of the table; but our friends, better informed, took up said article and proceeded to demolish — not the waiter, but — the stick; and French bread, we must acknowledge, is good, if it does stand uncovered in all public places and pass through all manner of transportation.

But of all strange things in this strange country, the strangest is the spending of the Sabbath day. Some people do not work, but if not, they usually play. If the doors are closed to business, it is usually because the employers and employed are in places of amusement.

We can say but little of the straight-forward honesty of the French people; of one thing, however, we are sure — whenever they could get a few sous out of American pockets their consciences allowed them to do so. A gentleman whose knowledge of French consisted in "*Cinquante centieme beef-steak*," drew forth a handful of the coins of the country to allow a guide to satisfy himself, and every piece of it instantly disappeared. In a small store where room was scarce and goods were arranged on high shelves, a purchase was made and the wrong change returned as usual. The customer was indignant, and made use of all the French at command to convince the merchant of the dishonesty of the transaction, but he deliberately ascended some steps used for the purpose of taking down goods, and seated himself on the topmost one, coolly surveying those standing below, and at the energetic threat, "*Je ne patronize vous*," he burst into a loud laugh, and they left in disgust.

There is more in this city of Paris than we could visit in three weeks of 1873 and in six of 1874, and more that we visited, improving nearly every day of the time, than we could think of telling our friends about; but some of the excursions to the environs are too interesting to omit. Four miles will be considered by many a long distance for a lady and little girl to walk, but we did it more than once to the Bois de Boulogne, and there met those who preferred to go by the *chemin de fer Americain*, (American street-cars,) or by one of the many omnibus lines going in the same direction. We have before this taken our readers from the Arc de Triomphe eastward to the Tuileries, now we will start from the same point and go in an opposite direction through the Avenue de la Grand Armée to the Porte Maillot, one of the seventy gates by which we can leave Paris. Probably an officer stands there to scrutinize us closely, but the innocent need not fear, so we walk through, paying no attention to his keen glances. We are already just upon the border of the ancient wood — Bois de Boulogne — four miles long and two miles wide, enclosed in its entire length between the fortifications of the gay city and the river Seine, which winds about like a serpent, as if loth to leave so much beauty and pleasure. And we wonder not that the rays of the heavenly bodies and the water of earth's river should travel to this point with the children of men, for here is wherewith to please every nature and every mood, from the quiet scenes of the wild wood to the festive ones of fashionable life. Soon after we entered the precincts of the wood we noticed an enclosure, for admission to which a few sous must be given, and then we were in the Jardin Zoologique d'Acclimatation, where every plant and animal under the sun may find a home. Even the dogs of all lands had their kennels in close proximity, but they did not have their liberty, or some of them would evidently have left when a darling little French poodle came into their neighborhood at the heels of its master, for no sooner had it appeared in sight than every canine, up to the bull-dog and blood-hound, ran to the limits of his wall or chain, then lifted up his voice and barked. What a concert! We have heard of "Bedlam let loose," and we are sure that said poodle thought he was in the midst of said region, for he was too frightened to stir, and was borne off in the arms of his owner.

The Aquarium is a building fifty yards in length, so constructed that no light enters except from the sides through fourteen reservoirs filled with water, in which the curious ways of the finny tribes may be studied, and as we walked through the entire length we seemed to be, with the famous French writer, Jules Verne, many leagues under the sea.

Approaching one of the picturesque lakes, we saw a natural prejudice toward color acted with all the dignity of the race of swans. Several noble looking specimens of the forementioned genus, but of the species

Niger, came sailing toward the shore with too much haste to be graceful, and stepping quickly upon the grass, ran far from the water's edge, while in the distance appeared a single grand Cygnus moving majestically over the waters, with snow-white plumage all erect and neck curved in proud disdain. A single step upon the land, and seeing the fugitives beyond her reach, she left them in entire possession and returned to the water from which she had driven them.

To complete the feeling that we were in all parts of the world at the same time, we stood where all sorts of beasts of burden and equipages were in readiness to accommodate the traveler in this part of the Bois. Two mammoth elephants gave their backs to the foreigner, whose names, Romeo and Juliet, showed that they came from beneath Italian skies, and we were told that they were a gift from the King of Italy to supply the place of Castor and Pollux, who were eaten during the late siege of Paris, together with most of the animals then accumulated. Camels from Algeria kneeled for their riders and shook them unmercifully, lifted up among their peaks. An ostrich from the desert bared its breast to the harness and presented the unique spectacle of a two-legged horse. All kinds of ponies and donkeys from Java and India and other remote lands completed the conveniences for being borne through this forest, and we pedestrians walked back to our Parisian home.

Another day we went almost directly across from the Bois already visited to one which began even earlier to send its legends down to coming generations. The Bois de Vincennes contains more than 2,500 acres, (we hardly need to say it lies without the walls.) The chateau dates back almost to the middle of the twelfth century and comes along up with the centuries until it is now a fortress, containing within its walls, nine feet thick, an arsenal, barracks, etc., watched over by the same grim old donjon, rising one hundred and sixty feet in the air. Exercising the rights of independent women of America, we ascended the five stories of this only remaining tower of the nine original ones, and looked upon the "playful Marne rippling merrily along" till it joins its sister, Seine, and, clasped in each other's embrace, they enter the "city of gardens" in the southeast part and pass frolicking through the most beautiful portion, having their waters, about a sixteenth of a mile wide, bridged twenty-seven times. Mirabeau, the Duke d'Enghien, and Madame de Pompadour, with a host of other historical characters, passed in procession before our minds, and the Bois de Vincennes became a new place unto us.

A day in the cemetery of Pere Lachaise showed us the resting-place of persons of note and the interesting tomb of Abelard and Heloise, with five beautifully sculptured steeples, fourteen columns and ten arches, formed from the ruins of the Abbey of the Paraclete, which Abelard founded and of which Heloise was the first abbess. Here was practiced the novel method of renting a burial-place for from one to five years and then giving it up to other occupants.

One of the most interesting of churches was St. Denis, four miles from Paris, the burial-place of the kings of France from Dagobert, in 580, to Louis XVIII. It stands on the site of a chapel built for the remains of St. Denis, who was beheaded for propagating the Christian faith. Down two flights of stairs we came into the presence of the old in death. The statue of Mary, Queen of Scots, kneeling with uplifted hands, stands by the side of her husband, Francis II.; but where is her body? The father and mother of Charlemagne lie here, but only the sarcophagus in which the great emperor was buried at Aix la Chapelle, for his body was found there sitting in its tomb. Napoleon I. intended to lie here surrounded by those of his dynasty, but others planned differently when they sent him to St. Helena.

After many more excursions which it is impossible to describe, on the 13th of August, 1873, we left for a season the beautiful city which had been our home for three weeks, with two faces upon our shoulders, one looking backward with regret to the joys behind, and one looking forward with delight to the pleasures before us.

The principal point of attraction to us was the Chateau of Fontainebleau, so after a two hours' ride in a southeasterly direction we came to another stopping-place on the banks of the same Seine, and in the midst of a magnificent forest over sixty miles in circumference and containing from forty to sixty thousand acres of wooded land, interspersed with little white villages where artists paint and rusticate. A neighboring city, Melun, is mentioned by Cæsar in his Commentaries, under the name of Melodunum, so doubtless the great general has been here before us, but on a less peaceful errand. The origin of the name of this forest seems to be a somewhat contested one, but the oldest form was *Fons Blialdi*, the Fountain of the Cloak, in reference to a hidden spring of water. It is said that one of its royal occupants, Henri IV., dated a letter, " From our lovely wilderness of Fontaine Belle-Eau." The chateau is composed of buildings of different epochs grouped around several courts, and we entered it by the one long known as the Court of the White Horse, from the statue of a horse moulded after that of the statue of Marcus Aurelius on the Capitoline Hill at Rome. It is now called the Court of Adieux, because here Napoleon bade his soldiers farewell on the eve of his departure for Elba. Passing through the long line of rooms, all of which are a sort of geographical museum, we saw the table which bears the inscription, " The 5th of April, 1814, Napoleon Bonaparte signed his abdication upon this table in the king's study." The ghost of Marie Antoinette haunts this scene as it does many spots of historical interest in the land of France. We pass through her *chambre a coucher*, and the adjoining one, her dressing-room, where the window fastenings were made by her husband's own hand, out into the garden, where the Chasselas grape covers a wall of a mile in length. The carps rise out of their watery beds with mouths, too large for beauty, stretched wide open for the crumbs we bring with us. A long walk through the picturesque forest carpeted with brown heather, and another refreshing sleep before we take the cars for Dijon.

Shall we stop to tell you of the old church where the Jacquemars rang the bell, or go to Lyons and wander between the Rhone and Saone, flowing side by side through this old city, where Claudius and Caligula were born, (there certainly is not time to talk about the manufacture of silks, although many people may be interested in that subject,) cross both these streams and ascend the heights of Fourvieres, or, higher still, up to the dome of Notre Dame de Fourvieres, and, if the day is clear, get the first glimpse of Mont Blanc?

SWITZERLAND.

Chapter VII.

OUR newly-adopted watchwords are "On to the mountains," so on we go, and before we are aware of it the mountains are reached. The country is magnificently wild, the peaks rise higher and higher around us, and we ever and anon dive into the depths of the mountain beds, and in darkness the minutes lengthen out to hours. But darkness comes upon us by the going down of the sun, and a heavy shower waits upon us into the capital of Switzerland. The borders have been passed by simply repeating the word "Americans," and a bow and a smile bid us God speed.

After the first rainy day in Europe, (the first that has overtaken the United Three,) a tour of observation is begun out of the city into the country. Yes, out of Switzerland into France, to visit the home of Voltaire. Who would ride when the roads are like the floor, smooth and clean, the roadsides grassy and decked with flowers that remind us of home across the deep waters — dandelion, thistle, spearmint, and the darling little Flirt Robert, that always brings before us loved faces of yore; the hedges, inviting and green, ofttimes loaded with tempting berries; who would ride, if they had health and strength to walk? Not we. The guide-books say that a fine view of Mont Blanc is to be obtained somewhere on this route, so with one eye over our shoulder, for we know it is behind us, we set out. All of a sudden, between the green poplars, a vision bursts upon us. Could it be aught but a vision? Could anything earthly put on such an appearance of the everlasting hills in the realms where foot of man never trod? Just above the horizon, yes, up in the azure blue, the home of the clouds, appeared a creation like unto the clouds themselves in delicacy and whiteness, seeming to melt away at a breath of the wind and assume a new form at every change of the atmosphere. Two objects our eyes have looked upon which have seemed somewhat similar unto this — the National Capitol at Washington seen from the Potomac many miles away, and icebergs upon the ocean; but this is the grandest sight of all.

At Fernet, the home of Voltaire, were the faces of Washington and Benjamin Franklin seen for the first time on this continent, and the sight did our eyes good. From the garden a most enchanting view of Mont Blanc was again obtained, and it was enough for one day.

Another day, the junction of the Arve and the Rhone was sought, and found about a mile away. They flow quite closely together for a little distance, a long, sharp point of land separating them, each showing its source and its course. The Arve, coming from the mountains whose peaks are in the clouds, down through the fissures in the glaciers, bearing along dirt and sand and stone, bears the hue of cloud and stone, and rolls boldly along as if ready and anxious to encounter obstacles; the Rhone, washed in the waters of the lake which it has just left, comes smiling peacefully with a look of heavenly blue mirrored in its face, rightly called "the blue Rhone." And so they come together, the blue and the gray. The gray rolls out into the blue, just as in the ether above the fleecy clouds of Autumn are followed by heavy darker ones; and the blue yields not to the gray, but continues on its course all undisturbed, yet determined to gain the victory. The struggle goes on as far as the eye can reach. Standing at the point of contact, and watching this apparent struggle, we strive to recall the words of a touching little poem so familiar to us all, "The Blue and the Gray," and in imagination we see two armies before us in fierce contest; the waves become the din of battle in our ears, and also the smoke of the cannon to our eyes; the life-blood of brothers flows freely; but we remember the conclusion of the poem:

> "They sleep peacefully side by side,
> Yea, in one grave, the blue and the gray."

A week passed at Geneva, and we start for those mountains we have looked upon so admiringly, feeling somewhat afraid that we shall prove the truth of the words, "Distance lends enchantment to the view." At the appointed time we are at the starting point, and with alacrity we mount the ladder which takes us to the upper seats of the diligence, bound for Chamouni. Up, up we go, higher than we ever rode before, to the front seat of the coach, which carries about thirty persons, twenty outside and ten inside. (How we pitied those below!) Five horses, three in front and two in the rear, stand ready before the coach to bear us along. Crack! crack! crack! goes the whip, and we are on our way. Now we are in a place where we can look over those walls which have troubled us so much in Europe, and we gaze into pretty, flourishing gardens, much pleasanter to look upon than the walls which hide them from view.

The day is all that we could desire and the company agreeable. Some Frenchmen in the rear discuss in an interested manner affairs of state and the consequences of war; at our side some Germans talk of Deutchland in their own guttural tongue; in more familiar accents some English enumerate the virtues of their land and queen, and an American girl eulogizes the sweets of maple sugar. We are quiet, and wonder if we are not up in the Tower of Babel.

We leave the beautiful little city on the lake in the background, and drive through little old towns and villages, through a country beautiful, more beautiful than parks. The mountains grow higher, more bold and craggy, till finally Mont Blanc completes the picture.

Everybody tells of fleet-footed children running after the carriage a long distance, and with extended hand begging for a pittance. We heard below us a sound like the mewing of a kitten, and looking down, there was the identical little beggar, with red cheeks, blue eyes, and flaxen hair, pursuing the coach at the top of her speed, and keeping up with it too, holding out her father's hat for the sous which she might receive. But it was not merely pretty little girls who asked for alms. There were great foolish boys, whose faces showed that they had not sufficient intelligence to care whether they received aught or no; and old blind men led by a child or dog; a mother with a neck larger than her head, and carrying in her arms a pitiably simple child. The scenes are intermingled, not all lowly and disgusting, not all glorious and sublime.

Our ride for thirty miles from Geneva, nearly all the time by the side of the Arve, was very enjoyable; but at mid-day the sun beat down upon us, and our seat was too high and the movement too fast to examine all the points as we desired, or to distinguish the genera or even the order of the numerous botanical specimens scattered in profusion about us; so we descended from our elevated position and became pedestrians. Then we were independent, and provided with note-book, guide-book, writing materials, Botany of Switzerland and French Testament, who could enjoy the remaining twelve miles to Chamouni better than we? Mont Blanc is straight before us, they say twelve miles away, but we feel like the little girl of our party, who is ready to argue the point, saying it cannot be more than half a mile away, for there are the footsteps in the snow. We shall soon find out, however.

Not only the people of this land, but of all lands, for they seem to be represented here, should bless the name of Napoleon for one good he accomplished — the making of splendid roads in this otherwise wild country. The Nicholson pavement of our cities is no better, the hard stony pavements not nearly so good.

The pines and poplars are everywhere, fences are few, and if a cow chances to be in sight, it is with a bell around her neck and some old man or woman at her side watching every mouthful she takes. Where are the men of Switzerland, while the women are raking the hay, driving the mules, caring for the babies, and cooking the meals? Perhaps they are making the beds, as we found strong, healthy young men doing in Paris; or perhaps they went to the war and never came back again. Where, too, are the lovely little Swiss cottages of which we have seen so many models? We have looked for them wherever a building was visible in the fields and among the trees, but instead we have found a dwelling-place for man and beast under the same roof, with better accommodations for the latter than the former, and an unmistakable animal odor pervading the entire premises. But we continue the search for the pretty Swiss cottages. Was ever road so beautiful, so romantic, as the one we pursue? Winding in all directions at the foot of towering mountains, and high above that frisking, leaping, passionate little stream of whose end we have already told you, and which we have learned to love by following it in its wanderings, as the mother does the wayward child.

We took one interesting meal during this our first walk among the Alps. "A word to the wise is sufficient," so we had provided ourselves with a spirit-lamp and materials for preparing a lunch should circumstances require it. Just at the hour of noon we came upon a wee cornfield, a few stalks growing up fresh and vigorous from among the stones laid down perhaps to draw the heat of the sun, and we asked the farmer to sell us an ear or two of corn, which he very kindly did. Sitting down by a spring on the roadside, with the rocks so high that old Sol could hardly get a glimpse of us, and the Arve playing the wildest music away below out of sight, and the long line of mountains in front of us bearing the name of Tete de Napoleon, from the fancied resemblance of its summit to the profile of the Little Corporal, we had our lamp trimmed and burning, and our corn cooking, while we sat lost in admiration and awe. We were suddenly brought to our senses by falling raindrops glistening in the sunshine. The romance was gone, and we were soon gone too; our fires were extinguished, and with provisions in hand we were seeking a shelter. We soon found a Swiss — not cottage exactly, but al least a house, and knocking at the door, a woman opened unto us and cordially invited us in French to come in. We explained the state of things, and she gave us permission to finish our repast then and there ; so, on the dirt floor, with the bare black walls about us, and the odor coming to our nasal organs which showed that the cattle occupied the same house at least a part of the year, we dined on our corn and black bread procured of the woman, (should have had milk also, but the goats had just been driven to the mountains in search of greener pastures.) The shower and the lunch were finished at about the same time, and we continued on our way. The sun sets at four o'clock, and we seek shelter, after a walk of six miles.

Of course we have bread and honey for breakfast, and then continue the walk by the side of the Arve. Gladly would we paint the bright, starry specimens we saw in that walk — the same heather we saw on the Bens of Scotland and in the forest of Fontainebleau ; the same yellow papilionaceous blossoms we have seen in all countries on this continent, and others of the same form of corolla, white, purple, blue and yellow, which turn to us such expressive faces that they need no words to tell interesting stories ; the lovely species of viola which we have seen in no country except Switzerland, (what violet is not lovely ?) with the tints of the sky and the sunset ; the delicate campanula, and the varieties of composite and labiate plants. And we would not stop our painting with the flowers, but would present to you a lovely landscape, taken at the hour of twilight, within a narrow valley, the vale of Chamouni, a most perfectly rounded basin of green grass, not one solitary shrub or tree or building, only a velvety green basin, dotted all about with trees and white houses; the Arve flowing around these, bringing the color and the air of the hills; the cows winding their way along, each and every one ringing its bell incessantly; a little higher up on the mountain side a circle of pines, dark and green; then streaks of snow and dark rocks intermingled, but soon an entire mass of snow and ice; still above, in the face of the young moon, slender as she ever appears, yet giving promise of light, the crimson clouds heaped up after the manner of the mountains, fading away into the grayish blue dome of heaven, directly above the grassy basin below. No picture is complete without some sign of animal life, so in imagination you may add to this the wandering trio who are threading their way through the romantic vales and glens.

We had walked about seven miles and a half from St. Gervais to Bellevue, and spent the night at a lonely wayside inn. Pursuing our way toward Chamouni, we met some of our English friends who had continued with the diligence to the end of the route, and were now retracing their steps to visit the Glacier des Bossons; so we walked several miles along the road, through the fields and up the mountain side to cross this glacier, which is in full view of Chamouni. Alpenstocks and socks are the first requisites for the passage. Then the question was solved which we had propounded to ourselves so many times, as to why the Swiss women were always knitting. Everybody who visits a glacier must have a pair of socks, women at least, and men must have nails in their boots, and everybody is expected to wear out the socks crossing once, so the Swiss women must knit or other women cannot cross glaciers.

If you can imagine the ocean in a terrific storm, waves mountain high and yawning chasms between, suddenly frozen, then you have some idea of a glacier. It is a frozen river coursing down between the mountain peaks, extending in some cases miles before it becomes a stream of running water merely. It is no easy matter to climb over these icy waves, and often we are reminded that the icy fetters are broken down between these waves and that the water has started on its course to the sea ; so we tread more carefully these peaks above, that we may not be plunged into the waters below.

The first glacier crossed, we climbed the precipitous banks, and just at the edge of the ice gathered the blue gentian and other bright Alpine flowers. Men are not alone in contradicting themselves, but nature too plays strange freaks. We spent the night with the *guide de chef*, Balmat, (the same in name and occupation, if not in person, as the one to whom Tyndall so often alludes in his journeyings among the Alps.) In the morning we reached Chamouni, August 28th.

Chamouni! Champs munies — fortified places ; name given doubtless with reference to the natural fortifications, the everlasting hills which crown the sides of the valley, two miles wide and fifteen miles long, highest of which is Mont Blanc. To obtain a view of the face of this queen of mountains, with her numerous attendants ranged all about her, we ascended first to an opposite peak, La Flegere. It was impossible to go up the steep mountain path in a straight line, but necessary to follow a zigzag road which made the way many times as long. Having ascended high enough to be in the clouds, was it strange that thunder burst upon our ears? There was no Swiss cottage to which we might retreat, so, improvising a shelter out of our waterproofs, we stood the storm as patiently as might be. The thunders rolled about us and the lightnings flashed below us, and we felt that we had gone beyond our sphere. The rain did not entirely cease, and we began to fear we should lose our journey, but walking upward in faith nevertheless, we at last found ourselves at the end of the route and in the sunshine above the clouds.

ILLUSTRATIONS.—1. Chain of Mont Blanc as seen from La Flegere, opposite. 2. Source of the Arveiron from the extremity of the glacier Mer de Glace. 3. Chamouni, at the foot of Mont Blanc. 4. The American Girl with her alpenstock.

What a position for mortals! Two rainbows spanning the clouds through which we had passed, and which showed us occasionally through their rifts the vale of Chamouni, and, higher still, that long chain of mountains so brilliant with the sunshine that it was truly golden, and suitable for the adorning of her majesty, the White Queen. Time was fleeting and the scene was changing, so we commenced our downward course at a very rapid rate and continued it just as rapidly for the space of three hours; and we slept well the following night.

On the third day in Chamouni we visited the Mer de Glace. To reach this so-called sea of ice from Chamouni, one must travel about four hours up the mountain's side, around and around, backwards and forwards, (most people ride on mule-back or are carried in chairs,) until the summit of Mountain Vert is reached; then begins a descent among boulders and rocks and stones and pebbles and sand — it seems as though the world had turned to stone.

One can see all sorts of bodies of water on and within this Mer de Glace; there are straits and channels innumerable; there are quiet little lakes standing upon its surface and sleeping within its bosom; there are cascades and waterfalls down in the blue depths, so romantic that one involuntarily looks for naiads and nymphs with flowing tresses; then there are torrents and whirlpools that make the beholder shudder and draw back with affright.

Standing on this icy sea, we recall the words of Tyndall: — "The great agent which nature employs to relieve her overladen mountains is the glaciers. At its origin a glacier is snow, — at its lower extremity it is ice. The change from white to blue consists in the gradual expulsion of the air which was originally entangled in the meshes of the fallen snow. The snow which falls on the mountain tops is dry, and the first action of the summer's sun is to raise the temperature to thirty-two degrees, and afterwards to melt it. The water thus formed percolates through the colder mass underneath and is the first agency in expelling the air entangled in the snow. Although the sun cannot get directly at the deeper portions of the snow, by liquifying the upper layer he charges it with heat and makes it his messenger to the cold subjacent mass." And Tyndall tells us too whence come these water-courses in the glaciers :—" The crevasses are produced by the mechanical strains to which the glacier is subjected. They are divided into marginal, transverse, and longitudinal crevasses. The first is produced by the oblique strain consequent on the quicker motion of the centre ; the second, by the passage of the glacier over the summit of an incline ; the third, by pressure from behind and resistance in front, which causes the mass to split at right angles to the pressure." The same author says :—" The glacier has the appearance of a sea, which, after it had been tossed by a storm, had stiffened into rest. The ridges upon its surface accurately resemble waves in shape, and this appearance is caused in the following way : Above the Montanvert, (the point whence we descend to the glacier,) opposite the Echelets, the glacier in passing down an incline is rent by deep fissures, between each two of which a ridge of ice intervenes. At first the edges of these ridges are sharp and angular, but they are soon sculptured off by the action of the sun. The bearing of the Mer de Glace being north and south, the sun at mid-day shines down the glacier or very obliquely across it, and the fronts of the ridges which look downward remain in shadow all the day, while the backs of the ridges meet the direct stroke of the solar rays. The ridges thus acted upon have their hindmost angles wasted off and converted into slopes which represent the back of a wave, while the opposite side of the ridges, which are protected from the sun, preserve their steepness, and represent the front."

We could not realize that this seemingly solid mass was all moving at the rate of about one foot in twenty-four hours, the centre moving a little faster than the sides, the latter being retarded somewhat by contact with the banks; but as it is conclusively demonstrated by Tyndall on Glaciers, we are obliged to accept the fact as truth.

We decided not to cross this glacier, so two of the party sat down upon the banks and waited for the Teacher to run out upon the ice and see how it appeared. At first it was quite level and not slippery; after going a little distance the writer came in contact with one of the much-talked-of crevasses, and, full of curiosity, looked into its depths, where were, occasionally, immense rocks brought down from unknown heights. Passing quickly along beyond the point where the crevasse ended, she turned around and came back on the other side of the crevasse, which gradually enlarged, and all of a sudden she found herself where it joined with another, making one still larger. They were too wide to leap across for fear of falling into their icy jaws, so she was obliged to retrace her steps and go back to the shore the same way, where her friends waited in great anxiety. It was a beautiful sight to look upon the background and see the Aiguilles (needles) of different names, all white and pointing heavenward, as the magnetic needle points to the North Pole, and to trace the course of the three branches which form this main glacier, up among the mountain peaks. Just thirty minutes were necessary to retrace our steps to Montanvert by the steep winding path among the rocks, and we stood again on the elevated pasture prepared to return to Chamouni. We should have done what most people do, gone entirely across the Mer de Glace and come down the other side, had not the guide-books told us of dangerous paths for little feet to tread, (and large ones too, for that matter.) At Montanvert a small party, with their homes upon their backs, (for what is home without food and fire?) were starting with their guides for Mont Blanc, highest peak of the Alps, (15,780 feet,) but having no anxiety to go higher that day, we returned, in an hour and a half, to the interesting little village nestled under the shadow.

Bells in Chamouni told us several new tales. Once, the soft tinkling of scores of tongues broke our morning slumbers, and going to the window, the sight was a novel one — a hundred or so of goats, each with its musical accompaniment, having left their milk to feed travelers from all lands, were going in search of the pastures which should supply them again. Another time, joyous bells rang out, and then everybody greeted some returning heroes who had been victorious in their contest with snow and rocks. Imagine with what regret we left Chamouni, singing all the time the sweet Swiss song:

> "Chamouni, sweet Chamouni,
> Oh, the vale of Chamouni!"

By this time we had become practiced pedestrians, and Bradshaw told us that the most interesting way of reaching Montigny was over the picturesque pass of the Tete Noire, which was accessible by mules and could be done in nine hours. But mules are too slow and too obstinate, so the Three set out on foot, and had gone but a little distance before the clouds became thick and overcharged with rain. What a silver lining that cloud had we did not at first discover. We shortened our analysis of flowers and quickened our steps to find a shelter, which we unexpectedly, and joyfully too, did find at Argentiere, four miles from Chamouni. The day was not half gone, but as it was the last day of the week, we concluded to remain there over the Sabbath. Had it not been for friendly intercourse with congenial hearts across the sea, it would indeed have been a dismal day. The clouds settled down almost upon our heads, and the mountain peaks, which had seemed so near and looked so pure, had almost withdrawn themselves from the panoramic view. It was Switzerland without the mountains, and the charm was gone. But on Monday morning, the first day of Autumn, our eyes opened upon a gorgeous sight. A silver lining we said the cloud had, but we thought then it was a golden one. One bound to the window, and no sense of propriety or decorum could restrain the bursts of enthusiasm and the clapping of hands. Aladdin's palace never rose more suddenly than the palaces of the Alps had sprung from the gloom. Awestruck, we said with Coleridge:

> "Who bade the sun
> Clothe you with rainbows? Who, with living flowers
> Of liveliest blue, spread garlands at your feet?
> God! let the torrents, like a shout of nations,
> Answer! and let the ice-plains echo, God!
> God! sing, ye meadow-streams, with gladsome voice!
> Ye pine-groves, with your soft and soul-like sounds!
> And they too have a voice, yon piles of snow,
> And in their perilous fall shall thunder, God!
> Thou great ambassador from earth to heaven,
> Great hierarch! tell thou the silent sky,
> And tell the stars, and tell yon rising sun,
> Earth, with her thousand voices, praises God!"

Quickly attiring ourselves lest the vision should fade, we went hastily through the little Alpine village, where the women had collected around their troughs and tubs and were lost in gossip and the labor of washing, out into the fields to see the snow-clad mountains and find the Glacier des Bois, the source of the river we had followed so long—and the delight of the writer must have been somewhat akin to that of Dr. Livingstone when he thought he had discovered the source of the Nile. The source of the Arve was not found, but it was its twin, the Arveiron. Yes, just above Chamouni we found that the gay little river was blessed with two heads. We kept them both in sight a long time, and finally found one of them hidden under the rocks of ice in the Glacier d'Argentiere. A most beautiful sight it is where it breaks out from under the icy arch and goes tumbling along, as it tumbles all the way till it meets the blue Rhone. No arch of triumph is carved more beautifully or more thickly set with shining crystals. Transparent blue are the juttings of rock, and weird and dark the caverns whence the water rushes out. We pluck a bouquet from the midst of the rocks near the fountain head, and with sorrow we part from the waters which have given us so much joy. We shall doubtless find other rivers coming down from these hills of snow, but we shall never forget the Arve.

Another has described the termination of this glacier as "An enormous mass of ice twenty times as large as the front of St. Peter ; a magnificent palace cased over with the purest crystal ; a majestic temple, ornamented with a portico ; columns of several shapes and colors ; it has the appearance of a fortress flanked with towers and bastions to the right and left, and at the bottom is a grotto terminating in a dome of bold construction. The whole is so artistically splendid, so completely picturesque, so great and beautiful beyond imagination that the art of man can hardly produce a building so grand in its construction or so varied in its ornaments." Truly there is often much in a name, as was proved in the present instance. Among the Latin nouns declined in childhood was Argentum, meaning silver, so like unto Argentiere, where was disclosed the cloud's silver lining in the silver dome of ice and the silvery waters of the Arveiron, rushing forth as if glad to meet the sunlight, of which the silvery tones of memory will keep our recollections bright.

PASS TETE NOIRE TO MARTIGNY.— CASTLE OF
CHILLON.— LACUSTRINE CITIES.

CHAPTER VIII.

OUR meanderings in this mountainous land may seem somewhat unaccountable. From Geneva on the western extremity of Lake Geneva, we had passed into France when at the foot of Mt. Blanc, and now on our way to Martigny, we again crossed the boundary between these countries, but at what point we know not. It was enough that three American girls walked sixteen miles that day and came down at the foot of the Pass Tete Noire, rather late in the day and quite footsore. Morning showed us what we could not see at that time, the place where the monks find a home when they have passed many less years than threescore and ten, on the Great St. Bernard saving the lives of men, for they can spend but a few years so high above the world, and they come down to end their days in the valleys below. This is the place where many start for the Great St. Bernard, which is twenty-two miles away. We should have been glad to follow in the footsteps of Charlemagne, Fred. Barbarossa and Napoleon the Great, but we concluded to take more peaceful ones. Passing over the Dranse on a bridge so old that we imagined the armies of Charlemagne keeping watch over it, we walked a little distance in the valley of the Rhone, and then for variety, took the cars to Bouveret where we cut off in a boat the south-eastern part of Lake Geneva sailing across the waters of the Rhone (these waters are aristocratic and do not wish to mingle with common waters,) to the Castle of Chillon at Villeneuve. The Church of Calvin and the Castle of Chillon confront each other at the extremes of Lake Leman (Geneva).

Here we must pause, for the poet has pointed out the way. Going down into the depths of the castle and standing by the column to which the prisoner of Chillon was chained and around which he had walked till he wore down the earth, we plainly heard him say:

> "My hair is gray but not with years,
> Nor grew it white in a single night,
> As men's have grown from sudden fears;
> My limbs are bowed though not with toil,
> But rusted with a vile repose,
> For they have been a dungeon's spoil."

We seemed to hear him give his own history in the words of Byron:

> "We were seven who now are one.
> Six in youth and one in age,
> Finished as they had begun,
> Proud of Persecution's rage,
> One in fire and two in the field,"
> Their belief with blood hath sealed;
> Three were in a dungeon cast,
> Of whom this wreck is left the last."

They tell us that when at last Bonnevard was set free he ran back to his column and begged to be left there in his second home, and Byron makes him say,

> "I regained my freedom with a sigh."

Twelve miles we walked that day by the side of the bluest waters and under the bluest sky that we imagine earth affords. We had purchased pictures at Geneva with which to confront the artist, and defy him to take us where we could find such colors except in the hues of the rainbow or upon the artist's brush; but we nevermore say that the views of Swiss skies and Swiss lakes are too highly colored. Concluding to stop for the night, although the sun was high in the sky, we left our lake

Chillon

road and entered a village old and curious, and walked through its one street in search of hospice, or anberge, or hotel, whichever you wish to call it, but we discovered none, and so continued on our way. When we reached Lausanne at the very northern point of Lake Geneva, we hastily sought the baggage room and asked for stray sachels which had preceded their owners by ten days. Nothing to show for them, how would our sachels be known from those of all the rest of the traveling world? But taking us back through several rooms they hauled up the identical sachels and straps which had been so bold at the beginning of the journey and were still just as fearless though they had traveled alone. We had sent them from Geneva and were glad to meet them once more.

The second week in September the beautiful lake of Geneva was left behind to traverse the shores of a neighboring lake, where a short time ago Lacustrine cities were exhumed, and the mode of living of an early and a very different race of men was made plain by articles suddenly brought to light which had been hid for thousands of years. At Yverdon, one extremity of Lake Neuchatel, cars were exchanged for our old mode of advancement in this land of lakes and mountains — pedestrianism. Sky was bright and lake was blue, but, relics of the past, antiquities, our eyes sought everywhere. Order and quiet reigned, and we walked the streets scarcely seeing sign of life or meeting living being; but feeling convinced, nevertheless, that other implements of husbandry had been used in these fields, and that other races of men had occupied these houses than the ones made familiar by studying the records so lately found within the bosom of mother earth. We thought to find something at Concise, but were directed to a chateau some miles away, where it was said the exhumed articles were kept in store for the eye of the curious to see. A romantic walk through private fields bordered with shrubbery and watered with fountains, brought us to the walls of a castle which looked as if built to protect, but which we scarcely dared to enter for fear they were built also to incarcerate the unwary. The bell at the gate house was rung, the servant withdrew the bolts, and with a look of curiosity invited the "Three" to enter. Ushered into the court we made known our errand, and were informed that the lord of this manor had deceased, and that his collections were scattered among the museums of the land, some of them to be found at Neuchatel, whither we were journeying. Begging pardon for trespassing upon the quiet of this very quiet house, we departed, feeling somewhat uncertain whether we were pursuing the ghosts of the past ages, or whether the pursuit was on the other side ; but Neuchatel reached, we were convinced of our own sanity and also of the truthfulness of newspaper reporters and of letter writers for magazines, for our own eyes looked upon the instruments of warfare, many in number but very similar ; implements of husbandry, evidently not much in vogue during that hard age, and cooking utensils fewer still, as they probably took their food in the natural state. But we refer our friends to the libraries of those who keep pace with the discoveries of the times, where they will find accurate descriptions of the Lacustrine cities of Switzerland.

THE AAR AND THE JUNGFRAU.

Chapter IX.

PURSUING our route across the country to Berne, in that city of bears we first made the acquaintance of another dancing, sparkling stream, along whose banks we have since wended our way for many a day, and whose waters we have traced high up among their mountain beds. Berne, the capital of Switzerland, stands upon a rocky citadel and looks down upon the Aar surrounding it on three sides, but at a great distance below much of it. True to the teachings of William Tell, (we shall not try to believe that such a man never lived,) Switzerland is still a republic, and this city is the seat of the Federal Council, and all its operations are carried on in three different languages, French, German and Italian; indeed it was difficult to tell in which tongue one would be answered if he addressed a person in the street. German, however, had become perhaps by this time the language most generally spoken. It takes all sorts of people to make a world, and it takes all sorts of cities too, and Berne is a sort by itself. Some of the streets are arcaded, and one walks a long distance as if in a continuous line of stores. Through the centre of many of the streets is a stone channel in which the water rushes swiftly to the Aar. Then such curious fountains are everywhere to be seen, many of them representing the bear as performing some

ILLUSTRATIONS.—1. General view of the city of Berne surrounded by the river Aar. 2. The Ogre Fountain. 3. Clock Tower.

wonderful feat. In one, called the Ogre, monster Bruin is satisfying his appetite by destroying innocent children, of whom he holds great numbers within his pockets. On one of the clock towers a procession of bears walk around and strike the hour of the day. In all the Swiss carvings displayed for sale the bear acts a prominent part, plays the fiddle, carries match-safes on his back larger than himself, sits at table, etc., etc. Real live bears, too, climb a pole within their pit, and watch for the morsels which are thrown to them, or for the unwary who occasionally drop themselves into their paws. In short, everything impresses upon the mind that the name Berne is derived from some word meaning bear, for what reason we cannot tell exactly, although we have heard many solutions of the matter.

When we leave the society of the bears and take a somewhat elevated position, we are fascinated with the view which rises before us. The silver horns rise up in plenty and the sun gilds them till they are like unto diamonds of the purest lustre — Schreckhorn, and Faulhorn, and Wetterhorn, and Silberhorn — and over all the grand array presides the Jungfrau, (young woman,) whose white veil sparkles in the setting sun as if adorned for the bridal feast, but who ever remains cold to the addresses of adoring ones.

The Aar and the Jungfrau are by no means all that are interesting in a visit to this city, but we left them all to follow these two — follow them by land and by water, over mountains and through valleys.

At Interlaken we took up the march anew, and facing the Jungfrau, ended a good week with a most delightful walk up into the one street of Lauterbrunnen. What a glorious place to spend the Sabbath! Rightly named — nothing but fountains; for within reach of the eye ten waterfalls come leaping, bounding, pouring down the mountain side,

ILLUSTRATIONS.—1. Lauterbrunnen, with Jungfrau in the distance and Staubach Fall at the right. 2. Hotel at Handeck, on the Grimsel Pass. 3. Hotel at the summit of Furca Pass.

LAUTERBRUNNEN

AUBERGE DE LA HANDECK

HOSPICE DE FURKA

among the number the celebrated Staubach Fall, one thousand feet high, which the poet says is like the tail of the pale horse on which Death rides. So the waters pour constantly into this valley, which has not a particle of flat surface except the river Aar at its base, and the Swiss cottages deck the hillsides everywhere, while the Young Maiden looks ever down upon the scene, adding life and contrast by her presence.

High up on the right of this valley, so blessed with flowing fountains, is Murren, the highest village in Switzerland, so of course we felt challenged to extend our walk up there, and after a climb of three hours where even mules do not go, we met on our return lines of little boys playing the part of beasts of burden, and we wonder no more that they are called simple Swiss, since they must necessarily pay more attention to their heels than their heads.

On the following day we pursued our course toward the Jungfrau, taking the other side view of the same pleasant valley, and it lost nothing by this examination upon all sides, the test of true worth. It sparkled with new brilliancy when, after a half-day's walk, we stopped for the last time to look over the scene and impress it indelibly upon our minds to carry across the ocean the next year.

A deep, deep gorge lay between us and the glorious Jungfrau, whose white peaks were towering before us. A sound which seemed familiar broke upon the ear, and was attributed to a train of cars in the distance; but soon it came again, and this time near enough to see the smoke, for right before our eyes and thundering in our ears down the mountain side rolled the terrible avalanche. It was a glorious sight. No torrent ever rolled more majestically down, down to the depths. It came like a large body of water till it reached the top of the precipice, then all of a sudden it became a light, glorious cloud, which melted gradually away, and we felt that we had seen a vision. We slept in front of the same cold mountain, and our dreams were haunted by avalanches, and they were not all dreams either. In the morning the snow came down upon us, and we wondered if winter had come to cut short our delightful wanderings. But we drew our water-proofs around us and ran down the mountain sides, (for we could not walk, they were so steep,) and after three or four hours we found it was not winter, only a storm of rain, and we went to our rooms in the valley of Grindelwald to bide the return of the sun. Old Sol did not withdraw his presence long, for early the next morning he was inviting his three friends out to visit the glaciers in the vicinity of Grindelwald.

It is a very up-and-down life this traveling in Switzerland. Four hours we had been approaching Grindelwald, all the time in view of her cottages; now again we were six hours leaving her with her glaciers in the valley; and again, with fingers chilled with cold, and getting somewhat anxious lest the bare mountain peaks must be our beds, we greeted with joy the noble St. Bernard dog which came out to welcome us to the chalet at the top of the Great Scheidig.

In the valley again, the Vale of Meyringen, an old friend appeared, the Aar, easily recognized, although somewhat diminished in size, and we walked by the side of this recovered friend until its tones were familiar as those of childhood, and we were lonely when they were heard no more.

For hours we passed on over a level but not straight road, just as good as labor can make it, winding around at the base of the mountains, following the windings of the Aar, until we almost came to the conclusion that a mountain pass was very different from what our inexperienced minds had pictured it. But wait! We have spoken of fearing that winter had come, but with the fervent sun pouring down upon our heads we came to a very different conclusion. At two o'clock, however, it was sundown, and we enjoyed the delightful long twilight hours. As we climbed, climbed, climbed, we could but say, How like to the journey of life! Away back in the distance were the beautiful days of youth, rugged and uneven, to be sure, but purple with the haze of time and gilded with the brush of memory. Around about us was middle life, struggle and labor and work and climb, precipices to avoid and heights to gain ; but far ahead was the sunshine, and perhaps we should get into it at the last. We were supported by this hope until the day's journey was finished, and we found a resting-place for the Sabbath, which was close at hand.

The Sabbath in Switzerland is a very different matter from what it is in some other countries. The little white church stood in the midst of the cottages, all huddled so close together that they reminded one of frightened sheep crowding around the shepherd for protection. At the proper hour the villagers came together, the women all wearing red handkerchiefs over the head, (except three unruly spirits whom fashion had led astray and placed the jaunty hat upon the young hair,) large woolen aprons, and a handkerchief tied demurely across the shoulders, the hymn-book held with both hands in the self-same position, completed the dress. Excuse a description of the elaborate attire of the other sex. Invited to occupy the one pew in the church by the old minister, who had filled its pulpit for thirty years, we listened to a good Dutch sermon on the very appropriate subject of Freedom. The services were conducted with the utmost decorum, and everybody seemed to feel the force of the truths presented and to live accordingly. This was the Swiss way of observing the Sabbath in the little village of Guttannen.

Another whole day's journey to the highest point in the route, past the Falls of the Aar to the Dead Sea. We were truly and literally in the region of the clouds, and thought the world had turned to stone. Oh, what bleakness and desolation — not a tree or even shrub growing ! But there was beauty there, and some flowers adorned even these rocks. We are told of the blue-bells of Scotland, but we can tell from experience of the blue-bells of Switzerland; about every inch of ground bears some species of the nodding campanula. Here, in the crevices of the rocks, in close proximity to snow, and provided by nature with a covering of down, they hang their heads, and ring their bells, and delight the weary wanderer. Then the stones and rocks were highly adorned with moss and lichens, so that the eye seemed to look upon a carpeted floor, whose groundwork was drab, but the figures always varying, always bright. But there was a little distance that the fog was too thick, the snow too cold, the water too deep, and the way too uncertain, to think much about flowers, if they were to be seen.

As we stood by the side of the Dead Sea up there, we were reminded that we might need a pillar of fire to guide us out of the cloud, for so dense a fog had suddenly enveloped us that we could not see our way but went blindly forward in what seemed to be the direction in which we had been walking, when we stopped upon the border of other waters rolling sluggishly along as if uncertain what course to take, stretched out and covering a wide expanse of rock and stone. There was not much time to deliberate, so we stepped into the floods, but they did not separate, and we walked through the head waters of we know not what stream or where it finds its outlet, whether in the Mediterranean Sea or in the Northern Ocean, or far to the East or in the West. On the other side we were no better off, but two remained standing on a high point of rock, and the third went off as a sort of scout calling to each other out of the mists. The one returned saying she had made a discovery which perhaps might be of advantage to us — a tall pole rising from a rock and a short distance away a similar one. So we went from pole to pole, and if we had gone in the opposite direction we should have come out at the Haspice of the Grimsel, where we could have spent the night and seen the sun rise high up among the clouds; but we came out of the cloud, which was our pressing desire just then, and as we descended to the village below we frequently looked back at the cloud above and rejoiced that the three had persevered and came down victorious, having been seven thousand feet above the level of the sea. Two armies once upon a time went up there to fight, and French and Austrian blood rolled down into the valleys below. Strange that they should not forget their feuds when they were so near to heaven.

Again we descended in zigzag course for about three hours and finally, near a place of rest as we supposed, we dropped upon the grass and waited awhile. After some enquiry for a hotel, we found this was a village where travelers do not often come and we were almost as much of a curiosity as if we had dropped out of the cloud, which was not far from the case. One woman was found who could speak French, who, with her four children, accompanied us a little distance and pointed out an inn at Oberwald, four miles away. Judging from data and our own bodily impressions, we had walked twenty-five miles that day. The next morning a few miles brought us to the Rhone Glacier. Tyndall looked down from the Mayenwand upon the Rhone Glacier and writes: "I hardly know a finer of its kind in the Alps. Forcing itself through the narrow gorge which holds the ice cascade in its jaws and where it is greatly riven and dislocated, it spreads out in the valley below in such a manner as clearly to reveal to the mind's eye the nature of the forces to which it is subjected. Longfellow's figure is quite correct; the glacier resembles a vast gauntlet of which the gorge represents the wrist; while the lower glacier, cleft by its fissures into finger-like ridges, is typified by the hand."

"It is difficult to convey any just impression of the scene from the summit of the Finsteraarhorn. The various shapes of the mountains, some grand, some beautiful, bathed in yellow sunshine, or lying black and riven under the forms of impervious cumuli; the pure white peaks, cornices, bosses and amphitheatres; the blue ice rifts, the stratified snow-precipices, the glaciers issuing from the hollows of the eternal hills and stretching like frozen serpents through the sinuous valleys; the lower cloud-field — itself an empire of vaporous hills — shining with dazzling whiteness, while here and there grim summits, brown by nature and black by contrast, pierce through it like volcanic islands through a shining sea;— Finsteraarhorn monarch of the Bernese Alps."

Why should the struggle between the blue (Rhone) and the grey (Arve) be so long and so fierce when their source is similar and their end the same? It can only be accounted for by the difference in their course and the impressions received from different surroundings. As we walked with one to the very beginning, saw it issue from the rocks and take their color as well as substance along with it through all its ways and windings, so now have we traced the other to the point where it seems to come from the blue above, and to take the sky in its onward route, (although congealed in its first attempts). The Glacier du Rhone at its base spreads over a large extent of surface, and the waters come, not rushing and pouring from one spot, taking along everything that comes in the way, but as if there was abundance of time and abundance of room, slowly and surely entering upon the accomplishment of their task. The Furca Pass winds backwards and forwards on the mountain several times taking the traveler to the side of the glacier where he can scarce make up his mind to continue his journey, but stands lost in wonder and admiration, then away a long distance only to return and behold a more sublime and wonderful spectacle in the frozen peaks and icy chasms extending almost perpendicularly. But even the Rhone Glacier must be left. We toil on up the steep and reach the Haspice at the summit of the Furca Pass where we take our lunch eight thousand feet above the level of the sea and prepare to go down into the valley of the Reuss. The Three were not united this time for one of the number considered it sufficient exercise to have climbed to the summit of the Furca Pass;

so the two left their companion to proceed slowly on their way and make observations in that elevated region, until the diligence starting two hours later should overtake them and carry them down into the valley. But things are wonderfully uncertain even at this high state of attainment.

The morning's walk had been in pure, unclouded sunshine, but, the height attained and the descent but just commenced, the clouds rolled up from below, enveloping all things in their dusky folds, leaving but a few yards before the travelers plain to be seen and easy to be followed. So, for a time, they walked in clouds, — no, ran, for the road invited brisk steps, and as the entire view was obstructed and the flowers were hid by their vapory covering, there was nothing to detain or hold them back. As a consequence, the diligence lost two passengers that day, for the end of the day's journey was nearly reached when night and the diligence together overtook them, and Andermatt, which ends the best part of the St. Gothard Pass, was reached and the St. Gothard Hotel was made a resting place for the night in the valley of the Reuss.

Many of the valleys in our native land are beautiful — hardly to be surpassed in that respect, — and the mind of the writer often reverts to the central one of the Empire State where the Onondaga flows on to the lake past scenes made familiar by daily walks during a score of years, imagining familiar hilltops overlooking the valley, familiar dwelling places where the homes and hearts are sure to be open when the wanderer returns, and familiar and loved faces so many that we would not attempt to number them. Another valley — my native valley — no lovelier one will ever be found, for there the sunshine of happiness gilded the days of youth, and although snowy peaks interposed their cold heads, rugged mountain paths came into the march of middle life and yawning chasms suddenly broke the path, yet away in the distant future the sun is still shining and the valley is beautiful — but not the valley of the Onondaga or the valley of the Tioughnioga, but the valley of the Reuss was the subject. Pardon the digression.

In the vicinity of Andermatt, somebody seems to have thought that his Satanic majesty has held sway at some past time, or perhaps does at present, for the bridge bears the name of Teufelsbrucke (Devil's Bridge). Once within that region we were led to doubt whether it was in the past that this dominion was acquired when the rocks were hurled in the wildest confusion and the stream poured madly through the narrow rifts, or whether it was even then that the contest was going on, for the clouds rolled up and over and around the spot, as if some of the scenes in "Paradise Lost" were being re-enacted; the wind almost lifted the garments off us, and we scarcely dared advance for fear of meeting the contending hosts. This was the wildest of all spots yet seen.

1

THE HOME OF TELL.

Chapter X.

AGAIN the windings of the river were seen, as several of the rivers of Switzerland have been, and by a gradual descent in the midst of the same delightful scenery, we came down out of the mountains where for two months the sunshine had been constantly on our pathway, and where we loved to linger still, but dared not lest the cold winds of autumn should drive away the pleasant impressions already received. In the loveliest days of the year, the hazy, musing, dreamy days of Indian summer, (for Indian summer is whenever these days come,) we entered the land so famous in song and story — the land of William Tell. William Tell, the hero of Switzerland, he who occupies the first place in the hearts of his countrymen, and who is still honored by every token of remembrance although centuries have passed since he gave to Liberty such a firm foothold in these lakes and mountains. During all these centuries,

> "True as the Alp to its own native flowers,
> True as the torrent to its rocky bed,
> Or clouds and winds to their appointed track,
> The Switzer cleaves to his accustomed freedom,
> Holds fast the rights and laws his father left him,
> And spurns the tyrant's innovating sway."

Into Altorf, a curious little Swiss town near the birthplace of Tell, where the houses were huddled close together after the fashion of the

---

ILLUSTRATIONS.—1. Statue of Tell at Altorf. 2. The Vow of the Rutli. 3. Tell's Chapel.

country, all standing right upon the street paved with uneven pointed stones, (they seemed,) so that it was doing penance to walk upon them, the trio entered with eyes extended to catch some sign of the hero of past ages; they peered at all the posts and glanced at the stones, looked enquiringly at the steeples and read the notices and guide-boards till in the earnestness of the search they became the centre of attraction, and were surrounded by numbers seemingly fearful lest their town was to be carried off bodily by the intruders; children and dogs barked till the smaller one of the party became somewhat alarmed lest the carrying off might be on the other side. But our motto is, "ever onward," and the search was rewarded by the sight of a statue standing over the spot where Gesler raised the hat, and where the apple was shot from the head of the son by the unerring hand of the father. Near by is a tower whose outside is covered with frescoes recording events in the life of Tell.

Curiosity satisfied at that point, the march was continued to Fluelen, at the extremity of the Bay of Url, whose waters were stirred by the oars of the hero; upon whose banks he leaped from the boat which was carrying him to captivity; and upon whose hillsides were made unfailing shots from the bow that sent the arrow to the heart of the tyrant. And we were permitted to look upon these places, so hallowed by association, this scenery, unsurpassed in grandeur and beauty even in this grandest of countries, and to walk nine miles at the foot of mountains from seven to eight thousand feet high, all the way on the border of the loveliest lake in Switzerland, the Lake of the Four Forest Cantons.

The Axenstrasse is nearly all the way cut in the solid rock, by the side of the lake, and is hard and smooth as the floors of our houses; it extends from Fluelen to Brunnen. At our backs were the snow-clad mountain peaks, hazy and blue at their base, but white and golden at their summits, giving all their colors to the waters below, while far away in the

distance, huddled in the curve of the lake, was the goal for which we were striving, Brunnen, and Schwytz, four miles above on the mountain side. Ever and anon we met droves of little dun Swiss cows, led by "Broon Lesel," which so gracefully wore her collar to which was attached a monstrous bell, followed by a "graceful ring" of bells and cattle to match them; all these were preceded by a mountaineer playing upon his Alpine horn, and following by another sending forth the Alpine cry. Who can imagine, who can tell the pleasures of the walk? And the Mecca of Switzerland lay in that route; yea, we visited it. At the foot of the great Axin rises a little chapel visited by pilgrims from all parts of the world — Tell's Chapel. It stands on the spot where the brave man, released from his fetters to save the tyrant Gesler from a watery grave, having seized his cross-bow, swung himself upon the plat,

"High springing with a bound, and sending back
The staggered boat from the whirl of waters."

An appreciative people raised this chapel in 1588, thirty-one years after the death of the one to whom it was consecrated, all the parties, it is said, having been his personal friends; and every year, on a certain day, a procession of boats laden with flowers, proceed slowly to this spot and deck it with wreaths — Nature's language of love. It opens upon the lake and bears upon its three sides ancient frescoes representing the principal events in the life of the hero whose name it perpetuates.

The shores of this most beautiful lake have witnessed other scenes in the history of Switzerland, dear to the freedom-loving Swiss as well as to the patriots of all lands where Freedom has had a birth and still lives to honor those who struggled to obtain it. At the extremity of the Axenstrasse, and also of that part of the lake called Bay of Uri, (for the name changes merely by a turn in the waters,) lies Brunnen, whose white houses had been the guiding star to the travelers from across the waters. This interesting little village faces Fluelen at the eastern extremity of

---

ILLUSTRATIONS.—1. Axenstrasse. 2. Monument of Schiller.

the Bay of Uri, and also Lucerne at the south end of Lake Lucerne, and it occupies a position only second to that of the last named place. Across the lake from Brunnen is the "Rutli of Schiller," where the "Three Confederates" wrote their names high on the roll of fame — so high that nearly six hundred years have not erased them — Walter Furst, Werner Stauffacher and Arnold de Melchthal. In the name of the three cantons which they represented, in the early morning hours and in the presence of thirty of their brethren, they took upon themselves the following vow : —

> "We swear to be one people of true brethren,
> We swear that no extremity shall part us;
> We will be free, free, as our fathers left us,
> Preferring death, in any shape, to slavery.
> And we Three,
> Firm, strenuous, without fear or guile, knit hearts
> And hands in one, so, warmed by our example,
> May the three cantons, Uri, Schwytz and Unterwalden,
> Join in like league, prepared like us to stand
> Or fall together, one in life or death."

How well the precepts and example of these brave men have been followed, even to the present moment, history will tell.

LUCERNE.

Chapter XI.

STEP with us on board the *Germania*, (it ought to have been the *William Tell*, but the time did not suit us,) and try the power of steam on this lovely Lake of Lucerne. Although the sun shone very warm upon us as we waited for the boat, once upon her deck and the wind was strong enough to overcome the heat of the sun, and we almost shivered as we went from one side of the lake to the other, to give each little town on its borders a call. In the broad noonday sun of an October day we landed at Vitznau to ascend one more mountain in Switzerland.

With reluctance we gave consent to be forwarded by iron and steam, and to heap up the raptures of this ascent instead of enjoying them moderately, one at a time. One large, broad car was filled, not crowded, and we started before an engine — yes, before an engine, for we backed up the steep mountain side. At first the curious engine, with its smoke-pipe perpendicular to the axis of the earth, (never mind, geographers, if this is not strictly true,) took the attention, but soon our eyes were drawn away from objects so gross and earthly, our view was enlarged, and our thoughts were elevated. One slope after another was ascended, one valley after another was laid out before us, and one lake after another was added to the scene. Think of this landscape, with a soft, hazy, dreamy atmosphere pervading everything and giving just enough uncertainty to objects to allow free scope to the imagination. Little misty clouds rolled together below us, and showed a silver outside instead of lining. One hour and a half was too short a time to take in so much beauty, but once at the summit of Rigi Kulm, six thousand feet above the level of the sea, and the panorama was laid out in one grand whole. Mount Holyoke gives a lovely view of the sister peaks of the Old Bay State and the winding Connecticut in the valley below; it is soul-inspiring to stand by the grave of the Father of his Country and look up through the valley of the Potomac, over the preparations both for peace and for war, halls of legislation and armed forts; Sterling Castle sends the mind roaming back through ages past, and recalls the bloody scenes enacted upon the thirteen battle-fields spread out to view, with the Forth winding and doubling itself in folds as if resolved not to leave these familiar regions;—but Rigi! Rigi presents the greatest variety of scenery, the most magnificent, the grandest. Almost without moving, we could look upon thirteen lakes of all shapes and sizes, dotted with innumerable little villages, green valleys, and mountain peaks too many to number or name, and all these encircled by the Alps bearing ever their crown of snow. Fortune certainly does favor the brave, for there are only a few days in the year when the beauty and grandeur of this scene can be enjoyed to such advantage as they were on the 27th of September, 1873. Oh, for the brush of the artist or the pen of the poet to portray the scene at the sunset hour! The crowd from the one large hotel which alone has the right to occupy this eminence were stationed for the grand display. If we had only been Argus-eyed we could have seen the beauties on all sides at a time, but, with constant turning, our poor weak eyes served us well, with the help of the artificial ones. As the sun approached the horizon, the clouds began to form in the depths below and to roll up one after another till trees and houses, lakes and valleys,

ILLUSTRATION.—Rigi.

Le Mont Righi.

UNIV. OF

hills and plains, were all submerged in one sea of cloud. The danger of being swallowed up by these waves seemed much more imminent than when upon the broad Atlantic. All around the far horizon were the mountain peaks, so white and wavy, so dim and hazy, or so red and fiery, that it was difficult to decide where earth ended and the regions of an entirely different nature, above and below, began. All too soon darkness covered the scene, and we went to our beds, as we had done many times before, mourning that beauty is so brief, and happiness so short.

At an early morning hour the Switzer's bugle call was heard in invitation to go forth and view the sunrise. The recollection of the gorgeous scene of the previous evening rendered a second call unnecessary, although the appearance of many showed that the toilette was not as carefully made as upon ordinary occasions. A large number of sleepy, shivering sight-seers stood at the summit, ready to be inspired when the proper moment arrived. But lo and behold! the lord of day drove forth his steeds under a canopy of clouds. What a blighting of hopes was experienced that morning! — for we had hardly yet learned that it cannot be all sunshine and no clouds. But the clouds were soon dispersed, and under the fairest of skies we descended the Rigi on our own footing, in the shade and in the dew — for it was not on the sunny side — and the Bay of Kussnacht was reached at the broad hour of noon, although an early morning hour had been taken for a start. Here again we were reminded that this was the land of the freedom-loving Tell, the tyrant-hating Tell; these were the peaks that echoed and reëchoed the brave Switzer's call to take a stand for liberty and for right; these were the plains where the bow was bent which sent the arrow to the heart of tyranny and destroyed it root and branch. On the spot where Gesler was slain the walls of a little chapel rise to tell the tale in all coming time.

Must we say that dreaded word which writes itself on so many things we love? Must we leave the brightest skies and the bluest waters, and clamber no more where the goat and the chamois make their home, and where alone is found the hut of the shepherd who guards the flocks during the short summer hours? Yes, it must be! Ye Alps, farewell!

The shores of the queen of lakes in Switzerland have been traversed in the sunny September days, in the beautiful Autumn days, and in the capital of the canton, Lucerne, we lay aside sachels and shawl-straps and linger a little in this city of light to examine places interesting to historian and geologist, as well as to all admirers of the beautiful and the true.

Perhaps the first object which attracts the eye, as we approach the city by the lake of the same name, is the picturesque watch-tower standing in the midst of the river Reuss. It was formerly used as a light-house, and gave the name to the city, *Lucerna*, (light-house,) but within its walls the archives of the city are now kept. Parts of the old walls are still to be seen, and some towers still stand, like the ghosts of departed ages. Other reminiscences of the past are also to be seen, and one can but feel that he is liable to fall into the power of the spirit of darkness as he crosses the Reuss on the old covered bridge, on which is represented the "Dance of Death." From whichever direction you cross this bridge, so old that it seems falling under your feet, you are confronted every few steps by the image of the grim skeleton whirling his victims of every age and every station off into other realms.

Then who has not heard of the Lion of Lucerne? Walking through the busy street, the scene changes, and the traveler stands before towering rocks as wild and grand as nature made them, with creeping vines upon their naked sides and tall evergreens standing like sentinels before them, and here, upon the rough rock, is the Dying Lion, modeled by Thorwaldsen, in memory of the brave eight hundred (less six) who died at Paris in 1792, defending the royal cause. This colossal lion, twenty-eight by sixteen feet, is represented as holding the *fleur de lis* in his paws and defending it with his last breath. The Swiss Guard will certainly not be forgotten while the rocks stand.

Just at the side of this famous rock of Art is quite as interesting a work of Nature — the Glacier Garden. Here is a book laid open in which is plainly written the record of ages past, of a time which printing and history have been altogether incompetent to reach, and of which the rocks alone give a true account. This little spot of ground, 112 feet in breadth, brings together times the most remote — a world teeming with life and activity, another with scarce a sign even of vegetable life, and in which there was no possibility of animal life. It puts desolation and plenty side by side — a winter that had no end, and an ever-varying change of season in which spring-time and harvest each has its appropriate time. It is the past and the present, and, as its name signifies, a union of opposites. This Garden, in the midst of the city of Lucerne, contains sixteen "Giant's Pots," the largest forty feet in diameter and as many in depth, containing several round stones, some almost as high as a man. In digging for a cellar in this locality the spade of a workman entered one of these holes, filled with soft dirt, and at the bottom the circular stones were found. Upon examination the sixteen were brought to light, and no building was reared on the spot, but the *debris* was removed, the matter was taken into consideration, and a satisfactory conclusion seems to have been gained, although there are some conflicting opinions. The Giant's Pots, with the rounded blocks of granite and limestone, are the signs of a time when glaciers covered the plain of Switzerland to the height of several thousand feet. These ice-streams flowed down from the heights of St. Gothard and brought with them fragments of the rocks, and as they retreated deposited these fragments in crescent-shaped hollows.

We could but fancy ourselves standing in this same quarter of the globe many (we do not attempt to say how many) years ago. Instead of Lucerne with all its bright attractions, its busy streets and crowds of men, its works of art and beauties of nature, our eyes look upon scenes made familiar only within the past few months. Our hands seem to grasp the friendly alpenstock, our feet to be covered with the socks of wool, and we are upon the blue glacier, looking down, down into the fearful cracks and numerous crevasses into which the little rills formed by the melting ice flow. We see huge stones lodged within these crevasses, as we have done many times of late, and now we see them set in motion by the water, and by this constant circular motion grind out the hollows in their rocky beds, and grind themselves smooth — perfect mills. Another work is going on, very slowly, at the same time. On the lower surface of the glacier is a layer of sand, and if in this layer there are large, sharp pieces of stone, they are pressed upon the rock in the slow but sure movement of the glacier, and form canals such as we see in several places in the Glacier Garden.

But the dream is past and we are witnessing the result and not the operation. A lane leads to a raised gallery, with cane seats, where we can sit and overlook the Garden, the Lion monument, a little building made in the form of the Bernese Oberland, in which is shown a relief of Switzerland, and a glass case containing rare relics of the lacustrine cities, those we found in our long walks and frequent halts upon the shores of Lake Neuchatel. All this within so small a space! We advise our American friends to visit the Glacier Garden of Lucerne, and if they have not as pleasant recollections of this bright, little seaport town, it will certainly be because they do not go there under such lovely skies, in the days when all nature seems golden and all the world at peace.

Another lake — Zug — another little town nestled under the mountains,

---

ILLUSTRATIONS.—1. Glacier Garden. 2. Lion of Lucerne.

UNIX, OR...

or hills rather, for the eminences seem considerably diminished, with its old cemetery, where is one remaining tower of the old wall ; and then another walk over the hills and by the side of Lake Zurich, surrounded with villages and vineyards. Passing a workshop, whence the sounds of labor issued, sounds of music struck the ear, a familiar strain,

> "Where are the friends that to us were so dear,
> Long, long ago, long ago ? "

We stood still. Where! yes, where! The broad Atlantic lies between us, the lands of foreign countries intervene, months of the past and months of the future lift up barriers of time. Is there anything else between us and our friends? We are just as near to those who have crossed the dark river of death as we were in our native land. " What a world of separation."

We have all seen many unequal matches in our intercourse with the world, but in Switzerland and Germany we saw a greater number in a certain time than ever before. On the highway was a large loaded wagon drawn by one horse and two of the genus *bos*, which gave unmistakable evidence that they supplied man with the usual accompaniment of the bread of natural life — one by the side of the horse, the other going before. We have seen a man, and also a woman, drawing with an ox, and many a time with a dog. A man was tugging up the mountain, with his wife upon one side and his little daughter upon the other ; but let it be to his credit said, that he bore the weight of the burden. We fear many are as unequally yoked in America.

Zurich offered attractions to the travelers sufficient to detain them within their borders over a bright Sabbath day. Another glimpse, almost a parting glimpse, of the beautiful, silvery Alps (we stop to gaze upon them wherever we can, for soon they will lift their heads no more for us,) the church where Zwingli preached, and the bow of William Tell, and then we hasten to the Falls of the Rhine. Full of curiosity to see this far-famed river, shall we be disappointed ?

To an American the word "falls" suggests our own Niagara, and no other is like unto it, a feeling somewhat akin to disappointment is liable to take possession of the sight-seer. If such should be our lot, we could not blame the weather-god, for he is still propitious unto us, still bestows most benignant glances and wears ever a pleasant face. Here we stand, upon the banks of the Rhine, just at the point where it flows over the jagged, uneven rocks, and sends out on all sides and at all times, flecks of foam soft and white as the snow of winter. Upon the opposite bank, too, is a chateau, the castle on the Rhine, which of course we expected to see, and which adds much to the picturesqueness of the scene. Within the walls of this castle is the place to descend to the foot of the falls, where one realizes more fully the beauty of the scene. It is indeed beautiful, but the falls are only about half the depth of Niagara, and the grandeur and sublimity of the deep high banks, the overhanging rocks, and the immense breadth of fall are wanting.

A walk of two miles on the banks of the Rhine brought us to Schaffhausen, a curious, very old city, which dates from the eighth century. Here we made ready for a sail on the Rhine, read about the famous castles on its banks, — one occupied by Queen Hortense and that son since so well known in the annals of France, another a prison for the reformers John Huss and Jerome of Prague, — and embarked with the early dawn. A heavy fog overspead the town, but that was not strange at so early an hour. We sat upon the deck and waited for it to clear away. On we went, growing somewhat impatient, for our time was precious; but that did not drive away the fog. The sun came up and gilded the mists a little, but they were too powerful to be dispersed, so we sailed on oh how gloomily! Soon the fog was so dense that the authorities deemed it advisable to warn any coming vessel that we were upon the track, so every few minutes a shrill wistle was sent forth, which did not quiet our nerves in the least. Disappointment had a firm hold upon us, and we sailed into the harbor at Constance none the wiser for having been upon the Rhine. The most tantalizing thing in the whole matter was that we had been upon the land but a very short time when the sky and air were bright and clear and beautiful.

When we landed at Constance, and with sachels and shawl-straps walked confidently toward a hotel whose doors we were sure stood open for us, of a sudden our ears were saluted with sounds that were altogether foreign, and we hastened forward paying no attention to them. Again they were heard and louder than before; yes, and from two different sources, and gendarme number one followed by gendarme number two, rushed out from a little office and followed after the sachels and shawl-straps and the United States girls carrying them; as if they thought Uncle Sam was being smuggled into their dominions and would cause commotion among the crowned heads. When we found that we were pursued we turned calmly around and delivered up the offending articles, saying "American." Charmed word! In a moment smiles wreathed the faces of the grim gendarmes and by motions they sent us on our way. We soon found that we were in the land we read about in the history of the Reformation, and Constance was interesting because the ashes of John Huss are mingled with its soil. Here one hundred years before the time of Luther, was this John the Baptist of the Reformation summoned to appear and condemned to be burnt alive, which sentence was executed after being imprisoned eighty-seven days. Just without the city an immense rock stands upon the spot, and the delicate Swiss violets waft the perfume of his holy life heavenward.

A dull sail on Lake Constance under leaden skies and a day's ride in German land in a drizzling rain, and we stopped at midnight where Luther came so prominently into notice more than three hundred years ago, went into the old church Saint Oolerie, which still stands a monument to the brave reformer, and then continued our way. Convinced that we had finished our traveling, for a time at least, not a day too soon, we gladly arrived at Munich, repeating the words of the poet,

"Wave, Munich! all thy banners wave!"

and upon the banks of "Iser rolling rapidly" we took up our quarters to live in Germany as the Germans live.

MUNICH.

CHAPTER XII.

AS we entered the precincts of this city after the warmer summer days had passed, even after that second summer whose days are so uncertain that we know but little of their beginning or their end, we could not expect balmy, pleasant weather, and if we had should have been disappointed. Rain and fog and gray and cold and bright followed each other so persistently that we were led to examine the records of the weather for years that are past — " 17 clear days, 127 cloudy, 221 alternate weather " — we must have fallen upon the latter, although they tell us there have been more bright days than ordinarily, and it has probably been like our own autumn days after all.

This city lies upon very level ground, supposed to have been a sea-basin, so far from the Bavarian Alps that only an occasional glimpse can be obtained, and that a sure forerunner of unpleasant weather. Munich lies upon both sides of the river. We find upon examination as to the origin of a city in this particular locality, that the land was owned by Monks, and that the first settlement was called " Forum ad Monachos;" this was more than seven centuries ago, but Munich was not a capital until a hundred years later. Ludwig the Severe was the first ruler, and in the very midst of this large city still stands what was at that time considered a very beautiful palace, built by the prince. It is closely surrounded by modern buildings of an entirely different style, and yet it looks as though it would stand for centuries to come, if assailed only by the hand of time. It is said to belong to the period of Duke Ludwig the Severe. It bears on its walls the date of its erection and also the name Alter Hof's (old castle). It was an object of great interest to us as it doubtless is to others.

Next to this castle in age are the towers of the old walls, erected before the close of the same century. The principal one is the Iser Thor, a fortified gate, consisting of three massive military towers. It is adorned with frescoes representing the battle of Ampfing, fought with the Austrians in 1322, and the escutcheons of the families who engaged in this conflict are painted around the summit. After the battle, Ludwig entered the town through this gate in triumph. There is talk at present of removing this old landmark from the place it has so long occupied, because it is a barrier to business and free circulation through the streets. How can the people consent to have so picturesque a monument of past ages taken from their sight forever? Must everything yield to the rush of business? Ludwig obtained the imperial crown of Germany in 1314, and reigned more than half a century, and when he was killed in a bear hunt, his remains were placed in the old Frauenkirche, although he had been excommunicated. When a new church arose on the same spot, a new monument of black marble was given to Ludwig, which is a prominent object in the principal church of Munich, the new Frauenkirche or Dome.

The entire house of Wittelsbach (the royal family of Bavaria) have been distinguished for their love for Art and Science, and they have caused to be reared many buildings which are still an honor to themselves and their city, and they have called to their court many men whom the nation and the world delight to honor; therefore Munich has long been not only the capital of Bavaria, but also the capital of the Fine Arts in South Germany, and her public buildings and parks show the statues of her heroes and celebrated men all along from the time of Albrecht V., of the sixteenth century, who collected the first cabinet of art. Four Maximilians have been of this family, and the fourth of this name assumed the dignity of King of Bavaria under the title of Maximilian I. His son succeeded, in 1825, and was called Ludwig I., the founder of new Munich. Under his administration the city, with its narrow, angular streets, suddenly became extended and airy and light. Immense palaces and buildings arose on all sides. As we descend one of the principal streets, Brenner-Strasse, we come to the Konig's Platz (King's Place) where are three buildings constructed by the influence of Ludwig I., which take us back to Grecian antiquity. These three buildings, the Propylæon, the Glyptothek, and the Exhibition Building, represent the three styles of Grecian architecture.

Ludwig placed his son Otto on the throne of Greece to deliver that land from the Turks, and to keep the matter constantly before the Germans he reared these three buildings in their midst. Without knowing aught of this fact, we felt as though we stood upon the soil of ancient Athens. The Propylæon stands over the street like a triumphal arch, and foot passengers go between the twenty-eight massive columns in the centre, while carriages pass upon either side. The Glyptothek, intended for the reception of antique sculpture, is one story high, and instead of windows has niches in which are placed, on one side, the statues of the protectors of ancient art, and on the other two those of the middle ages and the present time. We will not attempt to tell of the wonderful collections within its fourteen rooms, collections made almost entirely under the influence of Ludwig.

But the principal proofs of his industry and skill are seen in the Old and the New Pinakothek, the former for the paintings of ancient masters, and the latter for modern paintings. All the different schools are here represented in the fourteen hundred pictures. One entire room is filled with the works of Rubens — the largest collection of his paintings. The original "Beggar Boys" of Murillo is here, although copies are found everywhere. The work of the hands of Michael Angelo, Raphael, Titian, Tintoretto, Paul Veronese, and all others of renown, as well as some whose names are not known, are upon the walls. The New Pinakothek is a very strange looking building, with no windows, being lighted from above, and its outer walls covered with frescoes, as its inner are with paintings of modern artists, many of whom are at present living within this city. Nine hundred artists are among its residents.

These five wonderful buildings are only the beginning of the great labor which Ludwig performed. The Wittelsbacher palace rose as a residence for the heirs presumptive to the crown of Bavaria; two large wings were added to the royal palace; also the Ruhmeshalle (Hall of Fame,) designed for the busts of persons from all countries who have distinguished themselves by the work of hand or brain, of which ninety of life size are already in their places, within this hall of horseshoe shape. But this stands the largest casting in the world, the colossal statue of Bavaria, modeled by Schwanthaler, whose bust occupies its niche in the hall near by, and whose statues are everywhere to be seen in Munich. We went into the head of the famous Bavaria, but did not come out of her locks, as it is said twenty-six persons did on the day of her erection; but we sat upon the sofas up there, and looked through her eyes at the Bavarian mountains and the country round about. The metal of this statue, of which twelve hundred and eighty-four hundred-weight were used, was from cannon captured in war. The Bavarian lion stands at her side. A great deal more of such noble work might be mentioned as performed by this king during the twenty-three years of his reign. But the end was not so noble; for some misconduct he was obliged to abdicate the throne

---

ILLUSTRATIONS.—1. Statue of Bavaria by Schwanthaler. 2. New Pinakothek — Art Gallery. 3. Cemetery.

Bavaria.

Neue Pinakothek.

viiall

in favor of his son Maximilian II., and Ludwig occupied the palace he had caused to be reared for his heirs to the crown, before they had worn it instead of afterwards. Maximilian II. reared for himself a noble monument in the "Bavaresches National Museum." He said of it in his speech at the inauguration:—" It is an honor and example to my people," words engraven upon the frontispiece of the building. After Max II. came Ludwig II. and time alone will tell whether he will make for himself such a record as did the first of the same name, his grandfather.

The in-comings and out-goings of the "Independent Three," from their quarters on Schwanthaler strasse (very near the atelier and museum of Ludwig von Schwanthaler who did so much for Munich before forty-eight years of age when he died,) have been many. It would not be strange if they had caught some of the spirit of art everywhere so manifest, and they certainly will take across the ocean very pleasant recollections of artists, only two of whom they will take the liberty to mention. At the studio of Prof. Kaulbach we were delighted with the man at his work. More than seventy years of age, he still used the pencil and brush most gracefully, most successfully; and he bade fair to adorn many more palaces and museums, as well as private parlors, with the work of his hands, and also to adorn public and private places with a refined and gentlemanly presence. We shall remember long his pleasant face, his genial words, and his German Michael — the picture on which he was engaged at the time, representing the proud victories of the Germans over their neighbors the French, by the well-known features of Napoleon III., and his form lying prostrate under the steed of King William of Prussia. A few months after, in the sunny lands which we had sought, we learned with sorrow that he had laid down the brush and would paint no more, for cholera, the dread disease, had struck him with the chill of death.

For a two fold reason we love to mention a second artist, Paul Weber,— who became the teacher of one of the three, and enabled her to carry back to her native land beautiful views of Germany, and, by frequent invitation, he opened his home to the three without home and impressed upon their minds indelible pictures of a pleasant family in the Fatherland.

Almost seven weeks in München, the capital of Bavaria, each of our number having her hours for one of the three separate branches of study — painting, music, and language — and the remaining hours for a common purpose, we varied the time by study and amusement. We visited painting galleries too numerous to mention. In the public library, which is second only to that of Paris, and which contains 800,000 volumes, we saw Luther's Bible containing his and Melancthon's portraits, and the gospels written in gold and silver vellum, of the ninth century, beside many other interesting relics. We saw one custom carried out in this city which we never heard of elsewhere. As soon as Death claims a victim, the body is removed to a common receptacle, where it is prepared for the tomb, and lies exposed to the common gaze for a couple of days, in large rooms with glass fronts. With strange feelings we walked before these rooms for the dead, and saw all ages waiting for burial; there were several babes with sweet innocence on the face, there was childhood with the labor of life cut short, there was middle age with the furrows of care, and old age with the marks of distress or peace, according as Time had been cruel or kind; but all were covered with beautiful flowers, and the impression of disease and death as far removed as possible. We could but be glad we lived in a land where we could keep our loved till the earth covered them, and then look above for their home in the skies.

It did not seem to be the season of the year to learn to love lager beer, and besides it might be conducive to cholera for those unaccustomed to it, so the trio allowed others to carry the stone mugs filled to the brim and foaming with the loved beverage, and they took instead the coffee, almost equally loved by this people. Everybody knows that the coffee-houses are an important institution in Deutschland, but they can hardly realize how important till they have dwelt there for a time. They are the resorts of all classes and ranks and professions, at all times of the day and night; they are everywhere to be seen, inviting the hungry, calling the thirsty, tempting the laborer, and offering food and drink to all as economically as they could prepare them by their own fires. We are told that many laboring men and women set no table at home, but go always to the public cafés and restaurants, and that many of the servant girls receive daily their six kreutzers (four cents) with which they get their evening bread (abendsbrod) and beer or coffee. We see on the streets men and women working together, doing the same kind of labor, and upon inquiry as to the children, we learn that they are taken in the morning to a Retreat, where they receive care through the day and a dish of soup at noon, for a few kreutzers. It is very interesting to observe the way the people get their daily bread, and the great variety there is of this article of food. No one prepares it at home, but every one can be accommodated and supplied with what suits his individual taste. At certain hours of the day almost everybody is carrying in their hand or in a basket bread as though it were a baby. There is every shade of color and every quality of the material used. There is milk bread, egg bread, little horns, little snakes, braids, all-souls' bread, seamed bread, emperor seamed bread, caraway, coriander and salt seamed bread, (all these kinds very white;) then there is mason's bread, Romish bread, little black loaves and long black loaves, (the ones we see in the army so much;) these and many other varieties are made of flour; there is besides a dried-pear bread, made of dried fruits and nuts chopped and baked; and, to end with, Johannes bread, which is not bread at all, but beans, pods and all, sweet and nutritious. And every variety of this bread is good, very good, just as good as if made at their own firesides. There is certainly no trouble in finding enough to eat in Munich, if one avails himself of what is offered, and that too without making use of the national dishes, which are so seasoned and compounded that it takes time to learn to eat them.

Toward the end of November the threatening skies and cutting winds of Munich warned us out in search of warmer skies and milder breezes; so, on a genuine Autumn day, we again took up the line of march. Storm and rain, unaccommodating though they usually are, gave a farewell view of familiar peaks and towers, (Frauenkirche, Pinacothek and Glyptothek, Bavaria with the lion at her side and the uplifted wreath in her hand,) by taking a semicircle about the city, and we said good-bye to the Queen of Art.

INNSPRUCK.

Chapter XIII.

ON the boundary line between Bavaria and Tyrol (Germany and Austria) was an extensive fortification, which conclusively showed that these countries intend to be separate divisions, and are prepared for war as well as peace. Baggage was ordered up for examination, but the sachels and shawl-straps again walked through unobserved and unexamined, and that night we slept in the capital of Tyrol. The first beams of the morning sun bade us prepare for a lovely day, and with alacrity we obeyed. As soon as possible we were in the streets of Innspruck. Many times before during this trip of ours had we greeted snow-clad peaks in the distant horizon, lighted up by the morning sun, but never had we seen a city entirely encircled by them — a wall of snow and rock reaching apparently to the dome of heaven, in reality from six to ten thousand feet in height. A lace-work of silvery snow ornamented all these peaks, which contrasted most beautifully with the bright blue of the sky above and the sombre brown of the rocks below. The sun rose majestically over the scene and was clearly reflected in the waters of the Inn and the Sill, coming together just beyond the outskirts of the city.

Art, too, has assisted in making this place interesting. In the old Hofkirche, a church of the Franciscans, is one of the most splendid monuments in Europe — the tomb of Maximilian I. It occupies the centre of the church, is surmounted by a bronze statue of life size, and has twenty-four marble reliefs on the four sides representing the principal events in the life of this emperor. Twenty-four grim skeletons in armor stand in file on both sides like spectres of the past. Within this same church is the bust of Andreas Hofer, the William Tell of Tyrol, who met an end so unworthy of his bravery and patriotism. This monument perpetuates the memory of the Tyrolese patriot, but the bridge over the Inn, where the invading Bavarians were repulsed, and the Isal Berg, where the French were also driven back, are still more enduring monuments, and the hearts of his countrymen bear loving records which the hand of time can not efface nor the advancing ages crumble away.

One of the sunniest days of the year was that spent at Innspruck, and the pale new moon again looked upon us as we stood high above the city and came slowly down again from the mountain's side.

Thanksgiving Day in America — where were the wandering Three? Not in the circles where they were wont to be; not in the homes where they love to be. Did friends speak kindly of the absent ones? — wish they could taste the dishes so fondly relished in other days, and hope that next Thanksgiving they would occupy their accustomed seats? Going over the Brenner Pass! Well wrapped in cloak and shawl, we entered the car, where was spoken German, French, Italian, and the English which the Three carried on entirely between themselves. It seemed somewhat like a new edition of Babel. The only artificial heat received was from long flat pipes filled with hot water and placed upon the floor for the feet, which we found very serviceable. We started under clouds too, for the sunshine of the previous day did not extend quite far enough; but we did not forget to be thankful for the sunny skies of every land, from northern Scotia to the borders of Italy.

The first few moments took us through a tunnel out upon the borders of the Sill, which we followed for hours, up, up, to its very source, through tunnel after tunnel; for although we were going over the mountain pass, we could not go over all the peaks in the route. When we started the snow fringed the mountains above, but soon it covered the earth all about us, and everything seemed held in the icy hands of Winter. So complete was the change that we almost imagined some fairy's wand had waved over the scene, and all had been turned to silver. Threads of silver hung from the dark rocks, umbrellas of silver were spread over the sombre evergreens, silver carpets covered the ground, and silver clouds overspread the heavens.

With surprise we saw great numbers of houses everywhere, by the side of the railroad, on the highway, which during the entire route, lay in sight sometimes just with it upon a narrow space hewn in the perpendicular rock, on the mountain side, where it seemed that no foot could scale, and stranger than all, immense castles looked down from many a peak and seemed to bid defiance to invading hosts. We looked for castles on the Rhine, but saw them on the Brenner Pass. It was often difficult, however, to distinguish the pinnacles and peaks, the turrets and towers made by the hand of man, from those reared by the Master Architect; both make the traveler feel that he is passing beneath strongholds which time and force can hardly suffice to destroy, especially when the brave hearts of the Tyrolese, men and women too, are devoted wholly to the defence of the green mountains of the Tyrol. We passed near the spot where Andreas Hofer, with his small band of Bavarians, rolled the huge rocks upon the invading army, and rid their country of the foreign foe. Brenner, the highest point on this route, is 4,604 feet, the highest railroad in the world; and here the Eisenach issues from a little spring and commences its course toward the sunny plains of Italy, while on the other side of the street the Sill leaps over the rocks and hastens on to Austrian shores. Before we were fully aware that the descent had commenced, the winter of a day had passed and gone, the snow, where was it? Transient and passing away like a dream. But the spring was yet too young to put on her robe of green, she must bide her time in the nakedness of winter and store up strength for the seedtime and harvest, which will surely come. Bare and brown the trees extended their arms to the sun in the numerous chestnut groves; the mulberries, making ready for the food of the silkworm, that they may labor the coming summer for the lords and ladies of all lands; and the vines, climbing, clinging everywhere, and with all their little mouths sucking the sap to supply the luscious grape for the wine-press of man. Still the snow peaks were lowering in all directions, and every few minutes we stood at the window and gazed upon them, yes, bade them an affectionate farewell for fear they would be things of the past when we looked again.

At Botzen we waited for the light of another day to usher us into the realms of fair Italia, and were fully compensated. Great would have been the disappointment if the skies had not been propitious unto us. A brighter sun could scarcely shine upon travelers the last of November. Everything appeared to the best advantage; the red porphyry cliffs were brilliant, the old castle occupied by Dante in 1318, was illuminated by sunshine, even the marks of desolation made by the landslide which destroyed a city centuries ago, leaving only the stones to tell the tale, and the pen of the poet in Dante's Inferno — these were brought out in terrible distinctness.

As we came to the borders of the sunny land, the artificial heat was removed from the cars, the cold winds were left in the mountains, the skies threatened no more to send down snow and hail — we had found what we sought and went on our way rejoicing. Here a new difficulty arose; several times we addressed a fellow-passenger or conductor upon some important item, and in reply received only soft, musical, flowery sounds, sweet to the ear but unsatisfactory to the sense. English, French,

German, all elicited the same reply. Italian must be examined, so with Badiker's Conversationbuch we walk the streets of Italy, and by the way we would like to inform our many young friends that the study of the old dead languages, which they sometimes consider such a useless bore, is a sure, solid foundation for those with which they will come in contact on the European continent, and on the American also. Passing a fruit stand one day we observed a kind of fruit which was new to us; our look of enquiry was answered by "Apfelgranita." The course of reasoning was this: the German word "apfel" means apple, the Latin *pomus* means the same, making the substitution, the fruit must be "pomegranite," so we ate the angular crimson-seeded apple, as we have done many others since. Latin helped us out of that difficulty as it continues to do very frequently.

At the gates of Verona, and still the Alps stand by us, somewhat dim to be sure, but there nevertheless, white, picturesque, grand, majestic. Oh! what a pleasure they have been unto us, and their image, we trust, is engraved indelibly upon memory's page, and we shall turn to it often in coming days, and in imagination cross the glaciers, scale the peaks, tread the passes, and sleep in the green valleys of those beautiful mountains.

Now we are in the region of wars, ancient and modern, as the strong walls of the city we approach, would clearly prove. Fragments of walls we have seen in many places, but a city entirely encircled by them, in good repair, guarded and garrisoned, and ready for service, not until we reached Verona, in the northern part of Italy. The iron horse is not allowed within these walls; so, seated in the omnibus, we passed through the heavy gate, and a man in uniform took the liberty to put his head almost in at the window and cast a scrutinizing glance at Uncle Sam's three daughters. We felt almost that we were suspected, watched, and we certainly had a stifled feeling; the walls were too close, and in fancy we lived through some of the terrible sieges which the city, so near the dividing line between the two countries, has experienced. We heard the cannon thundering at the gates, and we shivered with fear as we imagined ourselves shut in by warlike hosts. But we were soon assured that peace reigned, and in security we walked the streets of this very old city, crossed and recrossed the Adige, and looked with intense interest upon the labor of centuries so long passed away.

First of all the old, old amphitheatre, so old that history fails to record with certainty its origin, claimed attention. With wonder and curiosity we walked around this interesting work of the ancient Romans, which in size ranks next the Colosseum, and which has withstood the shocks of time even better than the structure of the same kind at Rome. But it could not withstand the shocks of the earthquake; its huge walls were shaken so that only four of the twenty-two arches rise in their places to show what they were. We went to the topmost one of the forty rows of seats, and tried to imagine the twenty-five thousand descendants of Romulus rejoicing over the contests of men and beasts. Had we not fallen asleep over Livy, or Virgil, or Cicero as we prepared the lessons for Cortland Academy, and should we not soon find that the arena was what it had been so many years — a story and a dream? But day after day it continued to raise its blackened walls on the Piazza del Bra, and to face the old gate which has been standing sixteen hundred years, and which presents a double arch-way over the broad Corso Victor Emanuel; so the past and the present join hands in this land of the East.

When we extended our walks through the narrow streets and came suddenly upon the Piazza del Erbe, we could not with certainty say upon what times we had fallen, past or present, ancient or modern, barbarous or civilized, the abode of the living or the dead; here were indications of all times and of all kinds — most elegant palaces of marble blackened by age, but ornamented by art, statues of Catallus, Cornelius Nepos, Pliny the elder, and others of the loved sons of Verona, frescoes upon the outer walls, the column which once was proud enough to bear the famous Libra of St. Mark, the statue of Verona over the fountain, the tribune in the center from which criminals once received their sentence, — and beside all these, cabbages, potatoes, apples, oranges, pomegranates, in short, a modern market place in the ancient forum of the Republic — all the way from the sublime to the ridiculous. And close at hand in the public streets, above the heads of the living, were the sarcophagi of the illustrious dead, the princely monuments of a family of princes the Scaligeri.

Verona claims the honor of being the birth-place of one of the three celebrated painters of this vicinity whose works adorn church and palace everywhere in this land — Paul Cagliari, better known as Paul Veronese.

Again, as fast as steam will bear us, we go toward the shores of the sea. Time, too, is hurrying us away, and as the mountains rise in the distance, dim and shadowy, still suggestive of untold grandeur, fast going out of sight, so the days and the months of 1873 glide into the past, and soon their memory only will light up the journey of life.

VENICE.

Chapter XIV.

ALL brides are lovely, and all queens are beautiful, but where shall the words be found with which to describe the Bride of the Sea, the Queen of the Adriatic! The orator should be golden-mouthed, the writer should dip his pen in sunset hues, the reader should look with the eyes of bright fancy — even then Venice would not appear in a robe which is not her own.

The presentation took place in the last days of the year, when hearts were softened by passing time, minds were brightened by imagination's touch, the senses were enkindled by the fires of memory, and the whole being was alive to beauty and art. It was just at the sunset hour that we entered the realms of fair Venice. Never did gossamer and pearl more fittingly adorn bridal tresses; never did diamond glitter with more brilliant lustre in the bridal veil; never was the face of youth and beauty more brightly illuminated at the bridal altar, than the Italian skies on that eve of the declining year, by the rays of the setting sun. The colors of the rainbow encircled the horizon, shading from crimson through gold and green, and the bow was set with many a gem of light, such as earth fails to produce. All the brilliancy of color and light was repeated and

---

ILLUSTRATIONS.—1. General view of the Islands with the Grand Canal passing between them at the left. 2. Cathedral of St. Mark. 3. Square of St. Mark's, the column bearing the Lion of St. Mark and the Statue of St. Theodore; Palace of the Doges at the right; Palace of Victor Emanuel at the left; Clock Tower in front. The Campanile—Bell-Tower.

multiplied over and over again in the face of the waters, and the rays glimmered and danced and glided along as if hunting up each drop of the sea. There was not one cloud over this bright scene, and the feeling of the heart was, " See Venice and live."

Escorted by a polite French conductor, the sachels and shawl-straps were introduced to a German gondolier and the Three went out upon the streets of Venice. We made our èntree at the witching hour of twilight, and our first experience in a gondola was under a full, bright moon. Seated in this black carriage upon the waters, we passed swiftly along, feeling that we were attending our own funeral, so weird and ghost-like everything seemed ; on the borders of the Grand Canal the palaces of the past looked grim in their grandeur, around the walls on the lesser streams, the man in the moon played bo-peep until we were sure we were being spirited away ; and rubbing along between walls so high and gloomy, that we felt as if looking out of a deep well, we were convinced that we were being taken to that Bridge of Sighs, so fatally crossed in the days of yore. But this was only a moonlight view of the strangest of cities.

In and out, under and around, through and between, in all sorts of places, we entered finally a broad, open harbor, where the dreams of Venice were all realized. How could the human imagination draw a fairer picture? On every side out of the water the palaces of Princes, the spires of cathedrals, the domes of churches, the museums of art rose in the misty moonlight, and the Lion of St. Mark guarded them all. We anchored before an inviting home for wanderers, were welcomed by a genial German face, and slept as soundly as though we were not upon the borders of the uncertain deep.

The morning dawned as the day had waned, roseate and golden, and like charity, increased its own wealth by dispensing its gifts to everything around. Will our friends, one and all, accompany us on a tour of exploration, and observation — a tour of two weeks and a half in length? No shorter time will suffice; so every morning be prepared to commence almost with the sun, and stop not until his course is done. We started from an appropriately named hotel (**Aurora**) which faces the open sea, and the broad sun, too, rejoicing three of its inmates, at least, with bright light and pure air. You know full well that the domains of Venetia rise out of the Adriatic, not all together, but in one hundred and seventeen distinct parts, and that her lord, the sea, encircles them with loving embrace, which for centuries has not relaxed or grown cold. It is necessary for us thus early to make the acquaintance of our queen's consort, for we shall want many favors at his hands, and shall often avail ourselves of the skill and knowledge of his servants in visiting points of interest. Our first view, on this first morning, is of this same old sea, holding in his hands the wealth of his bride, and the flags of all nations wave proudly above him. We go out upon the street and walk over the broad pavement of the Riva del Schiavoin, crossing three of the three hundred and six pontes, over three of the one hundred and forty-six canals, all of which will become familiar to us. Here begins our acquaintance with Venetian life, superficial perhaps, and common, but such as we meet everywhere in these streets. People of all countries come face to face with us. The dress of all nations is displayed here, and the accents of all lands break upon the ear — one more familiar than all the rest often brings the Three to a halt on their march and sends an enduring glance out after the one whose tongue declares him of kindred birth.

But we have now come to a point where we must stand still and gaze — gaze and admire — admire and wonder. It is not strange that this people say :—" One Venice, one Sun, and one Piazza San Marco." The state entrance from the sea, where Cardinals and Doges and Kings are landed — and many common people too — is between two granite columns, one bearing the Lion of St. Mark, the other the statue of St. Theodore, the former patron saint of the city; and this is the entrance also to that famous piazza which ranks so high not only in the opinion of the Venetians but also in the judgment of all who look upon it. Nearly six hundred by three hundred feet in extent, paved with stones as smooth as our floors, surrounded by sumptuous palaces, ancient and modern, adorned with the work of all ages, in marble and painting, who can estimate the beauty and life and interest that center here? In the arcades which encircle it upon three sides, are the beautiful productions of this country in glass-work, corals, jewelry, and everything ornamental and gorgeous; on the fourth that palace so famous in the history of Venice, the Palace of the Doges, and the cathedral of St. Mark, equally renowned for its age, and grandeur, and relics, and for its famous horses, which have traveled from Rome to Constantinople, to Venice, to Paris, then back again to Venice. High above all this towers the Campanile, which Napoleon I. ascended on horseback when he conquered Venice.

And everywhere in this bright scene are the gentle, graceful doves, hovering, fluttering, alighting, their plumage variegated in the rays of the sun, purple, crimson and green, the pure white beneath their wings showing only when they soar aloft, reminding one of angels in beautiful disguise; when the whole flock, almost innumerable, take a sudden fright and all together rise in the regions of air, we seem to look up into starry regions, but they soon become falling stars, and settle again in our midst, again putting on the robes of earth. These doves are the property of the city, protected by its laws and fed on its bounty; and every day at two o'clock their dinner bell is rung and a sumptuous repast is served at the hands of one appointed for the task, assisted by numerous little boys and girls, provided with their soldi of corn. They are considered as guardians of the city, their presence giving promise that it will not be swallowed up by the sea, and they are said to join in the religious observances by flying daily three times around the city in token of the Trinity.

As we have walked through the Piazza San Marco one after another of these December days, in the midst of the scenes we have described, the sun shining with a clear bright light, the band playing lively Italian airs, the people sitting at the tables in the open place sipping their coffee, and the flower girls presenting their bouquets, we could but ask, how is it at Syracuse? Pardon us for being thus tantilizers, in drawing comparisons, but for one winter, at least, give us Venice.

We are not going to take much time and space to tell about the Church of St. Mark, with its forty thousand square feet of mosaics, some of them dating from the eleventh century; its six hundred columns, many of them bearing capitals brought from the church at Jerusalem; its two spiral translucent columns of alabaster from the temple of Solomon; the stone on which Christ stood when he preached to the inhabitants of Tyre; the one on which John the Baptist was beheaded; the relics of St. Mark, said to have been stolen from Alexandria and brought to Venice; — we are not going to tell of these, nor of the floor of white and colored marble, agate, porphyry, lapis-lazuli and malachite beautifully arranged, but so disturbed by the tread of feet and lapse of ages, that one feels as though walking on uneven ground; nor scarcely a word about the lack of windows and the consequent gloomy appearance of this church, for it is the famous cathedral of St. Mark.

We shall not say much about a structure perhaps equally interesting to readers and sight-seers, the Palace of the Doges, whose majestic and magnificent walls of red and white marble once seen can never be forgotten — the Hall of the Upper Council, one of the finest rooms in Europe, a suitable place of meeting for those whose names were written in the Golden Book of the Republic; the Hall of Scrutiny, for the forty-two noblemen who appointed the Doge; the Hall of Inquisition, whose ten chairs still occupy their places, stiff and stern, though their occupants have long since passed to their reward; and the Hall of the "Fearful

Three," around which dark memories hover that send shivering sighs through the form of the beholder, in vain sympathy for those who, centuries ago, appeared before this cruel tribunal. Just one word about the Doge's letter-box, the Lion's Mouth, which gaped so many centuries to receive its victims and send them with certainty over that fatal bridge whose end was death. It is there yet, open, but harmless; it bites not, for the teeth are gone. We crossed that bridge from the palace to the prison, looked into the rayless rooms where the condemned slept without a bed, saw the horrid preparations for disposing of the victims who stood in the way of ruler or accuser, and went back rejoicing that our home was in free America, our government an independent republic. This Ducal Palace and this Bridge of Sighs have been the theme of many a poet and novelist, and Byron and Dickens describe them in language all chaste and glowing.

Do not think that one day's sun is all that is necessary for that Piazza St. Mark, which is one of the finest promenades in the world;—that Cathedral of St. Mark, which was consecrated in the year 1111, but which has been adorned and beautified through all the intervening centuries, until it is filled and weighed down with the works of art and genius, the precious productions of Mother Nature and the wonders of the world; that Palace of the Doges, which Dickens says is more beautiful in its old age than all the buildings of the earth in the prime and fulness of their youth; the palace of the reigning King of United Italy, Victor Emanuel, which he keeps in readiness but never occupies— the palace of the present face to face with the palace of the past; the Campanile, the highest monument in Venice, which is ascended by an inclined plane, having one step at each angle as you go around and around up to the summit, and there look out upon one of the finest views in the world—distant, snow-capped mountain peaks, blue and misty realms on the face of the deep, and a city which belongs to both land and sea; the three standard poles which bore the flags of the conquered countries, Cyprus, Candia and Morea, when Venice was in her glory, the queen of many realms, but which now support the flags of the Italian nation; — no! day after day we pass through this glorious place, and every day adds to its glory, until our eyes are dazzled and our senses bewildered.

"A vision rises out of the earth, and all the great square seems to have opened from it in a kind of awe, that we may see it far away; — a multitude of pillars and white domes, clustered into a long low pyramid of colored light; a treasure-heap, it seems, partly of gold and partly of opal and mother-of-pearl, hollowed beneath into five great vaulted porches, ceiled with fair mosaic, and beset with sculpture of alabaster, clear as amber and delicate as ivory. And round the walls of the porches there are set pillars of variegated stones, jasper, and porphyry, and deep-green serpentine spotted with flakes of snow, and marbles that half refuse and half yield to the sunshine, Cleopatra-like, 'their bluest veins to kiss' — the shadow as it steals back from them revealing line after line of azure undulation as a receding tide leaves the waved sand — a confusion of delight, amidst which the breasts of the Greek horses are seen blazing in their breadth of golden strength, and the St. Mark's Lion, lifted on a blue field covered with stars, until at last, as if in ecstacy, the crests of the arches break into a marble foam and toss themselves far into the blue sky in flashes and wreaths of sculptured spray, as if the breakers on the Lido shore had been frost-bound before they fell, and the sea-nymphs had inlaid them with coral and amethyst. The St. Mark's porches are full of doves, that nestle among the marble foliage and mingle the soft iridescence of their living plumes, changing at every motion, with the tints, hardly less lovely, that have stood unchanged for seven hundred years."

Dr. Fish says:— "The story of the doves is that at the siege of Candia, in the thirteenth century, Admiral Dandolo had intelligence brought to him by carrier-pigeons which helped him to take the island, and that he used the same swift-winged heralds to send the news to Venice. From that day to this they have been protected, and thus they have been the pets of Venice for six hundred years."

We have traversed but a very small part of this city on the water, which extends about two miles from east to west, and three-quarters of a mile from north to south, having gone very little beyond this central point; but we will now extend our perambulations and walk through the Merceria, where the ladies go "shopping," the Broadway of this city, (it is hardly broad enough for three people to walk side by side in many places.) After turns and encounters numberless with the many going in an opposite direction, we come to the famous Rialto bridge which extends over the Grand Canal. Here we shall pause and consider the locality. The word Rialto (Riva Alto) means High Shore, and it was the name given to the central island, the oldest part of Venice. Near by we see the oldest church in Venice, founded in 421, and we look with curiosity upon the porch of Greek marble, which is about all that is left of the original building. From the Rialto bridge we look up and down the Grand Canal, the thoroughfare of the city, upon the blue sky, but a small part of which we have been able to see on our walk, and upon the busy scenes of commerce which continue to be enacted here as they were in the days of old. We remember that Shakspeare speaks of the merchants of the Rialto, but it was not to the bridge but the island that he alluded.

The Canalazzo, or Grand Canal, is from thirty to sixty yards wide, like the letter S, and nearly two miles long, the largest part on the northeast. The Grand Rialto is a high arch, with one central and two side flights of stairs, separated by a row of twelve shops on each side.

Byron says,—

"Didst ever see a gondola? For fear
You should not I'll describe it you exactly;

'Tis a long covered boat that's common here,
  Carved at the prow, built lightly but compactly.
Rowed by two rowers, each called gondolier,
  It glides along the water looking blackly,
Just like a coffin clapped in a canoe,
Where none can make out what you say or do.

" And up and down the long canals they go,
  And under the Rialto shoot along,
By night and day, all paces, swift or slow;
  And round the theatres, a sable throng,
They wait in their dusky livery of woe;
  But not to them do woful things belong,
For sometimes they contain a deal of fun,
Like mourning coaches when the funeral's done."

Through the one hundred and forty-nine canals, under the three hundred and six arched bridges of marble, the gondolas glide, and the cries, "*Stali!*" (to the right) and "*Premi!*" (to the left) come like songs to the ear, to warn those approaching of the danger of collision. We are upon the briny waters of the deep, that come and go with the tides of ocean through the narrow passages walled in by palaces, the difference between the lowest and highest tides being six feet three inches, and the average difference from two to three feet.

One of the peculiar institutions of this peculiar city is the water-carrier, who, with two brass buckets across her shoulder, (from which a little ragged urchin might steal a drink,) goes to the open square and fills them from the artesian wells with water brought from under the sea.

We did not forget the Bridge of Sighs, (Ponte del Sospiri,) which Byron tells us in "Childe Harold" was "a corridor divided by partitions into two narrow halls, one for political prisoners, the other for common criminals. Two tiers of dungeons, ten in each, the only furniture a pillow of stone, two feet long, fifteen inches wide, four inches high. The prisoner, when taken out to die, was conducted across the gallery to the other side, and then being led back into the other compartment of the

---

ILLUSTRATIONS.—1. The Rialto Bridge over the Grand Canal. 2. Bridge of Sighs. 3. Water carriers.

PONTE DI RIALTO

bridge, was strangled. The portal is now walled up, but the passage is called the Bridge of Sighs. Scarcely a ray of light glimmers into the narrow gallery which leads to the cells, and the places of confinement are totally dark. A small hole in the wall admitted the damp air of the passages, and served for the introduction of the prisoner's food. The cells are about five paces in length, two and a half in width, and seven in height." With candle in hand we followed the guide through all these dismal scenes, and we felt that the name was rightly given.

So we went day after day in different directions, until we had passed over the limits of the city, and visited very many of its ninety churches, remembering especially the ones which contained the tombs of the three most celebrated Venetian painters — Titian, Tintoretto and Paul Veronese. This city and this country is full of their works, and the land still rings with their praises. The tomb of Titian is decorated with a beautiful *bas relief* of his finest painting, the Assumption, and in the Hall of Fine Arts we see his first painting at fourteen years of age, his best at middle life, and his last at ninety-nine. Surely time and strength were given unto genius, and the three wrought a glorious work. In the same church with the tomb of Titian is the curious one of the sculptor Canova, modeled by himself, — a procession of the Arts following one of their number to the tomb, the Lion of St. Mark looking on with sadness.

During all the eighteen days that we were in the realms of fair Venetia continued sunshine brightened the face of our queen — pure, unalloyed sunshine, except in a single instance of a few hours, when the clouds encircled her brow; but they so soon passed away that they scarcely made an impression. Only one thing marred the pleasantness of our stay, and that was the constant applications on every hand for the administration of charity. The words we could not understand, but who could mistake the looks and gestures? No matter how exquisite the work of art we were contemplating, how grand the structure we looked upon, how lovely the skies at the sunset hour, or how fervent the prayer within the church walls, everything was interrupted by the meagre hand, the pleading eyes and the wailing tones of all ages. It was terrible; and we must recommend the Queen of the Adriatic and the King of United Italy to devise some means by which the land shall be rid of this dreadful scourge of beggars.

Venice is amphibious — a mermaid or sea-nymph. The lower part is a fish, but above the form is human. Like Venus, it sprang up self-creative from the froth of the sea. The Veneti took refuge from Attila in these islands of the sea and began to build a city after the Roman empire had fallen. It was married to the sea every year, but the cunning Venetians instead of wasting their treasures dropped the glittering bauble into a net carefully spread for the purpose, in which it was fished up to be used in the ceremonies of successive years. The ring was of gold and gems as large as one of those huge door-knockers that in former days gave dignity to the portals of great mansions.

There must always be something sad connected with our recollection of every place; so in Venice there was a picture which left its impress upon our mind — the parting of the Doge Marino Faliero with his heart-broken wife when he went forth to be beheaded — a traitor — and in that palace of pictures, in the midst of the 122 Doges, we remember the frame that was without a Doge, only the bare board to look upon, not even a name.

Three delightful weeks in Venesia's 117 islands (three large and one hundred and fourteen small ones), and it seems that almost every inch of Russ pavement in her 2,194 streets from six to twenty-five feet wide, of her 297 squares, of her 387 bridges, and her entire circuit of seven miles, all this, or nearly all, must have been wandered and wondered over by

---

ILLUSTRATIONS.—1. Horses of St. Mark. 2. Titian. 3. Tomb of Canova. 4. Tomb of Titian.

the Three. (The strangest sight we saw in that locality was one horse.) We have said it was continued sunshine in Venice, and so it was; but at the parting hour, when grief always dims the bright luster of the eyes we love, and sorrow clouds the brow of cherished friends, is it strange that the face was darkened and the tears were just ready to flow? We could have wept ourselves as we bade farewell to " Beautiful Venice," the Bride of the Sea, and steamed across the 2 1-2 miles of railroad whose foundations seemed to be sliding into the deep. Once again we stood upon terra firma. New faces and new scenes are all powerful in driving sadness from the heart, when it is not deep-seated, and in a comfortable frame of mind we arrived at the depot outsides of the walls of Padua.

There, before that triangular city, the mind seemed lost in the midst of ages, going back even to the destruction of Troy, when Antinor, the brother-in-law of Priam is said to have founded Patavium (Padua); coming up through the darker days when barbarous hordes held sway under Alaric and Attila, and on through the brighter age of Charlemagne, up to the time when the princes of Carrara ruled and reigned therein. Intensely interesting was the oldest city in northern Italy — interesting with its narrow, crowded streets, its long lines of arcades, which leave one almost in doubt whether he is walking within doors or without; its university so celebrated just at the dawn of literature after the sombre Middle Ages, when scores of names were enrolled in the book of fame by the side of Dante, Petrarch and Harvey; its hundred churches — San Giustina, with the tombs of St. Matthew and St. Luke, and moreover, the remains of three thousand martyrs down in the depths where a light is kept constantly burning and where we were invited to cast our eye, St. Antonio, magnificent beyond description, with its eight ponderous domes overhead and the great bronze crucifix of Donatello in its presbytery; Eremitani, which contains all that is left of the princes of Carrara, the lords of Padua, the tombs of two of their number; the Piazza Vittoria Emanuel, the only public promenade, with its encircling stream of water and two rows of statues representing Padua's celebrated sons; Botanic Garden, the most ancient in Europe, and the house, bearing record that it received Dante when he was exiled from Florence. Does one doubt that all this and much more renders Padua interesting in the extreme?

But we visited Padua especially to look through the eyes of an artist friend at a famous little chapel constructed and ornamented for princes by the hand of one who then was young but afterwards became famous and still lives in the hearts of appreciating admirers although centuries have passed away — Giotto. We found this chapel where we never should have thought of looking for anything beautiful, surrounded by other buildings and behind an old high gate, at which our guide rang for admission. We tried to look with an artist's eye, but we shall not attempt to use an artist's pen in description, but shall refer our friends to Murray's account of this wonderful Giotto's chapel, and we shall go on to places which are perhaps less interesting but easier to describe, only saying that Dante was the artist's friend, and that he was with Giotto during the work and probably suggested many points. The statues of the two friends stand side by side in front of one of the halls of Padua.

After two days at Padua we resumed the line of travel, taking cars for Bologna and passing the birthplace of Livy, the home and burial place of Petrarch, also the very ancient town of Adria, which gave its name to the Adriatic Sea, but which is now far from the harbors of those waters; and other places interesting for their associations in art and literature.

Having arrived at Bologna in the dark hours of a winter evening, (Italian winter) the first care was for bodily rest and then in the morning for Bologna sausages of course, followed by a survey of the town. Another old city is before us, which was founded by the Etruscans and called Felsina, conquered by the Greeks and named Bononia, (old coins bear the words "Bononia dreit,") united to the possessions of Hannibal, and converted into a Roman colony, all many years before Christ. We have said it was Italian winter time, and so it was; for when we left our hotel by the side of the depot and entered the walls, the mist and fog shrouded everything, and gave it a very uncertain aspect, so that we could well believe and realize that its foundations were laid deep in the ages of the past, its walls were reared in days that were dark, and its towers were in the mists of time.

But mist and fog did not prevent our walking in the boasted University, almost the oldest in the world, where ten thousand students were at one time assembled, where the anatomy of the human frame was first taught, and galvanism was discovered by Galvani, and where numbers of our own sex have occupied the professors' chairs, one of them so beautiful that she must needs lecture behind curtains that she might not distract the sound minds or turn the stern hearts of her listeners of the opposite sex. Wonder of wonders! beautiful and learned, and a woman!

We were not hindered from visiting several of the one hundred and ninety churches, a way which we soon learned by the attracting (not attractive) cries of coachmen and guides. The most interesting one is St. Petronius, which was intended to be the largest church in the world, but lacks the honor, owing to its still unfinished condition, and which contains the head of St. Petronius in a silver vase; St. Dominius, founded by that saint, who was also the founder of the Dominican order of monks, and containing the tomb of the saint crowned by a statue of the same from the hands of Michael Angelo, and beautified by an exquisite little angel of white marble, wrought by the chisel of this master sculptor, (this church also contains the tomb of Guido Reni); and St. Stefano most curious of all, a pile of seven different churches constructed at different periods on the site of the ancient temple of Isis, built on different levels and fitted up according to the time of their erection; among these, the round church of St. Petronius containing the body of that saint without his head, is modeled after the Holy Sepulcher ; the second contains a model of the vase in which Peter washed his hands and the cock which crowed three times, and in the crypt is a pillar which is just the height of Christ.

The fogs did not obscure the brilliancy of the pictures in the Academy of Fine Arts, where were displayed many of the productions of the artists whose home has been in this city, but whose fame has spread through all cities — the Caracci, Francia and Guido Reni. One of the latter was specially interesting, as it brought to mind a tale which is told concerning it, which is somewhat after this sort :—The master was painting the crucifixion with his model before him bound to the cross, and in the frenzy of the moment the knife was sent to the heart of the victim, that the death agony might be faithfully portrayed on the brow of Christ. The artist fled after the task was done, leaving his work to find him out, which it did after a few days ; for years Guido Reni was an exile, but his fame procured his pardon, and Bologna and the world honor the artist, although a murderer.

Neither fog, nor mist, nor cloud prevented our ascending the leaning tower of Asinelli, immortalized by Dante's likening a well-known prince in the infernal regions to this tower with its leaning summit enveloped in clouds. Around and around within this dark wall of brick, with no particular order to the arrangement or length of the 447 steps, having no inner wall like most of the high places we ascend, only a railing which is enough to prevent the climber from going down into the dark open space, preceded by a boy who lighted a match every few steps to illuminate a little, up we go to the very summit and out into the open air for a view of the city. But here the fog and the mist are all powerful to blind our eyes, and not an object can we trace except the roofs so close to our feet that were we on a level with them we could touch them with our very hands. There comes to mind the familiar lines,

> "Hearts are broken, hearts are turned
> With castles in the air,"

and we think how many times in life we have been lured to some eminence by brilliant castles in the air, but have turned back with hearts almost crushed with sad disappointment. Time will tell us how the leaning tower of Bologna compares with the one of which more frequent mention is made, in the land of Pisa, whither we are journeying.

FLORENCE.

Chapter XV.

WE turn our course toward the "Fairest city on earth," the "Athens of modern Italy." Who does not know what city is thus honored with appellations of great promise to the traveler? Florence, fair flower of the garden of Italia! On Christmas day, 1873, we entered her limits. Truly she is fair, for this land of age and tumults; fair for this country where the blossoms of peace are so frequently trodden under foot by the mailed heel of the warrior; fair, indeed, for any land or age or time. The first form which the eye can distinguish is that dome of domes, the largest in the world, towering high over the entire city, and admitting the rays of light upon the tombs of two of its architects — Giotto and Brunelleschi.

We can easily trace the " Golden Arno as it shoots away

> Thro' Florence's heart, beneath the bridges four;
> Bent bridges, seeming to strain off like bows,
> And tremble while the arrowy undertide
> Shoots on, and cleaves the marble as it goes,
> And strikes up palace walls on either side."

The Arno, silver stream of interest that it is, flows the entire length, enriching its fair possessor with its liquid wealth, calling to mind the most powerful picture we met in our travels, called "Bathing in the Arno." A number of soldiers were enjoying the luxury of a bath, when, alarmed by the approach of the enemy, the fright and the hurry and the confusion which were apparent in the faces and positions of the nude bodies will always be suggested by the river Arno. Six bridges cross its waters, over the oldest of which six centuries have glided as the currents have glided beneath its arches, and neither time nor floods have availed to remove its foundations as they have those of the remaining three constructed in the same manner

There are two suspension bridges of modern date. One of the bridges, the Ponte alla Carraja, was broken down in a fire in 1314, and from the terrible struggles of the drowning in the floods, Dante conceived his idea of the Inferno (which, by the way, was read with great interest by the Three while in the city of Florence). But the most curious and most interesting of these bridges is the Ponte Veechio (Old Bridge) or Jeweler's Bridge. It is lined by shops of jewelers and goldsmiths and other workers in metal; above these shops is a gallery connecting the Uffizi Gallery and the Pitti Palace, which, although inferior in extent to those of the Vatican and the Louvre, are probably the richest galleries of art in the world. This has been called " most melodramatic of passages." In following us through these galleries and halls our friends must sharpen their imaginations to the keenest point and then expect to fall far short of the beautiful reality which our eyes looked upon in the three long corridors, two 430 feet each, one 97 feet, and in the side cabinets and halls numbering 22, where the ceilings were frescoed, and there were ancient busts of eminent men, sarcophagi, statues and bronzes, medals, inscriptions, antiquities, vases and paintings, portraits of 300 painters executed by themselves, and a most splendid cabinet of gems.

We commenced in the Pitti Palace (the production of Lucca Pitti who strove to outbuild his enemy Strozzi) and many times we lost ourselves in these ages of the past, for we were in the halls of Mars, Saturn and Jupiter, and Appolla, Venus, the Iliad, and we were in the presence of the spirits of the past whose productions make this city a place of resort for artists from all parts of the world. Here was the Venus de Medici, "chef d'oeuvre of art, the beau ideal of beauty, the wonder of the world;" it was found in Adrain's villa at Tivoli, and generally attributed to Praxitiles 2,200 years ago, but according to the inscription on the base is the work of Cleomene, an Athenian. Here too was the Venus of Canova with a light drapery thrown around her, which instead of concealing heightens her charms ; and the Venus of the Bath, very properly occupying *une petite chambre* all by herself, except as the living curious step in to gaze and admire where everything is pure and white and delicate (it is no place for false modesty). The Madonnas were all about us — Raphael's Madonna of the Chair, which is found in almost all parlors of our American homes, and the manifold madonnas of nearly every artist of note, for each one had several, but Correggio's kneeling madonna was sweetest of them all, to our unartistic eyes, in the motherly pride and joy over her baby boy. From the walls looked down the Beggar Boys of Murillo, with eyes which almost brought the soldi from our pockets, the Four Philosophers of Rubens, and the Three Fates of Michael Angelo, so intent upon their work that we felt our thread of life slowly and surely drawn out and spun, and almost expected to see it clipped short by the scissors of the stern sister.

Not the least interesting among the curiosities of these galleries were the pen and ink sketches of the celebrated artists, composed of a selection from the 33,000 belonging to the gallery, the most remarkable being thirty-seven original drawings from the hand of the master artist Raphael. There were specimens too of the work called pictra dura, a mosaie which instead of being wrought and shaded with painted glass, is wrought in a tablet of slate and marble with precious stones of the natural color, the only manufacture of the kind in the world. One table employed

---

ILLUSTRATIONS.—1. Ponte Vecchio, Old Bridge, over the Arno. 2. Dante, Tasso, Petriarco and Aristo, crowned with laurel. 3. Correggio's Madonna. 5. Savanarola. Galileo. 6. Fresch in Giotto's Chapel at Padua.

twelve persons eight years, and cost 20,000 crowns. We came out through the fine portico of the Uffizi adorned with twenty-eight modern statues of celebrated ancients Giotto, Dante, Petrarch, Americus Vespucius, Michael Angelo, &c.

From the Piazza Santa Marie del Flora, rises that largest of domes, or broadest at least, which served M. Angelo as a model for St. Peter, and by its side stands the Campanile, rising "like a perplexed fine question heavenward ;" the walls of this bell-tower are of black and red polished marble, (those of the church are black and white) and are embellished with more carving than most cities have within their limits ; it was designed by Giotto in 1334.

Upon one of its six bells are the arms of the family so closely connected with the history of this city — the Medici ; another called the Misercordia was so named because it was rung when the services of that brotherhood, (which had an existence for 600 years) were needed. Close at hand is the Baptistry, which was built in the seventh century from the materials of an ancient pagan temple, — an octagonal building which has been made an object of wonder by the wonderful doors, which the wonderful artist said were worthy to be the doors of paradise. We stood before them many times and admired them beyond expression, and yet we prefer to imagine that the entrance into paradise is through a brighter, lighter gate at least.

On the same Piazza stand the statues of two of the architects of this world-renowned cathedral — Arnolfi and Brunelleschi.

Near by, a stone in the wall bears the words, "*Sasso di Dante,*" marking the spot where the immortal poet sat and watched the work, and encouraged his friends while rearing the disputed dome. We felt like following the example of the little one of our party, sitting against this seat in the wall to see if the spirit of the writer would not descend upon us.

Santa Croce, the Italian Pantheon, is interesting for the tombs of the great men who are buried here. Here lies the most illustrious of Florentines and one of the most variously accomplished men that ever lived — Michael Angelo, the painter, sculptor, poet, architect and engineer. Well may Sculpture, Architecture and Painting sit mourning over his remains. He died at Rome in 1563, but was brought to his native place and buried in the spot chosen by himself, so that when the doors are open he might be in sight of the dome of the cathedral, the delight of his life. Near by is the tomb of Galileo, the great astronomer, and also the tomb of Dante, "father of Italian poetry and advocate of Italian liberty," but his body is kept out of the reach of the city which so unjustly banished the Divine Poet. The ages are here brought together by works of different kinds, from that of Cimabue, the old, old painter, and Giotto, almost as ancient, to the struggle of the Italians for independence in 1848. (Two bronze tables bear the names of the Tuscans who died defending their land.) Pius IX. laid the foundation stone of the marble façade in 1857, and almost down to the present time (1865) Dante was given his proper place and his statue erected to guard the resting-place of Italy's noblemen.

But the finest of all the truly exquisite work in the beautiful city of Florence is the Medicean Chapel. It was planned by one of the Medici to receive the Holy Sepulchre, but as they failed to obtain possession of the latter, they made use of the chapel for a family vault. It contains most magnificent work in marbles and precious stones, and if their palaces while living compared favorably with those they occupy after death, we wonder not that one of them at least acquired the title of Lorenzo the Magnificent.

In the centre of Florence is the Piazza della Signoria, which takes precedence over all the other public squares for importance and antiquity,

---

ILLUSTRATIONS.—1. Cathedral Duomo. 2. Michael Angelo. 3. Cathedral Santa Croce. 4. M. Angelo's Three Fates. 5. Monument to Dante. 6. Tomb of Michael Angelo.

and the principal edifice is the Palazzo Vecchio, rightly named the Old Palace, for it dates from the year 1298. It resembles a fortress rather than a palace, and its peculiar tower becomes a familiar object, seen as it is from every part of the city and surrounding country. The bell of this palace was used to call the people to the public meetings; the palace itself was the seat of the Signoria of Florence. The Loggia is a sort of arcade, built in 1355 as a place for the magistrates when they wished to assemble the people. It is ornamented with several fine pieces of sculpture.

The Piazza della Signoria is doubly interesting from the fact that it was here that Savanarola, the Dominican monk, "stood among the ages, orphan of the old, prophet of the new, like Noah among the worlds of God;" here he endured the terrible torture of the hoisting rope, and gave his name to coming ages as a martyr for the church. We recall the description of this celebrated man by Mrs. Stowe:—"He was of middle age, of elastic, well-knit figure, and a flexibility and grace of motion which seemed to wake every nerve. The close-shaven crown and the plain white Dominican robe gave a severe and statuesque simplicity to the form of his figure. His low, broad forehead, prominent Roman nose, well-cut yet fully outlined lips, and strong, finely moulded jaw and chin, all spoke the old Roman vigor and energy, while the flexible delicacy of all the muscles of his face and figure gave an inexpressible fascination to his appearance. Every emotion and changing thought seemed to flutter and tremble over his countenance as the shadow of leaves over sunny water. His eye had a wonderful dilating power, and his voice possessed a surprising scale of delicate and melodious inflections."

Florence is truly the flower of Italian cities — neat, airy, and, most wonderful of all, has but few beggars. The surroundings seem to elevate all persons above the degradation which is so common in this country, and we could walk a few steps here without witnessing some disgusting sight or hearing some distressing sound. The environs are enchanting. Fancy us walking in a bright sun over one of the bridges, through the old town, and out from one of the gates into the country. We confess that we did shiver a little with the cold, or perhaps it was trembling with fear lest Winter should overtake us in our flight even now, for we saw some ice in the classic river and a good many snow-capped hills not very far away; but then, just at hand, as we walked toward the town where Galileo made his observations while he had eyes to see the heavenly bodies, were green bushes, bearing with the leaves both the flower and fruit. We said, "Surely Winter cannot come where Nature develops in this way," and Winter did not come. We saw the snow only on the hill-tops, as we had seen it all the past Summer. On New Year's Day the scene was brighter still. Two miles' walk by the side of the Arno to the Cascine — the most beautiful walk and drive in the world, they say. Oh, how lovely! Streams of equipages, crowds of people everywhere in the bright, warm sun. The heights of Fiesole we ascended, the city which was old when Florence was young; where the olive trees lined the walls rising one above the other, and the old palaces stood as they have done so many, many years; and where, once upon a time, Milton, afterwards the blind poet who saw Paradise Lost with the eyes of the inner man, met Galileo, the blind astronomer, who saw the earth revolve although the world was blind to the fact. What a meeting, and what a place to meet in! They were truly examples of the blind leading the blind, and after more than three centuries the world has at length learned to regard them aright, and to-day thinks more of the finger of Galileo, preserved in spirits and shown among the treasures of the

---

ILLUSTRATIONS. — 1. Podesta Palace. 2. Bell-tower of the Duomo. 3. Strozzi Palace. 4. Stairway. 5. Baptistery. 6. Palazzo Vecchio (Old Palace). 7. Loggia. 8. Bronze doors of Baptistery. 9. Riccardi Palace.

city, than it did, in the days when he advanced unwelcome truths, of the noble body with its undying mind.

Florence combines much that is old with the beautiful and artistic, and we left her, saying: " Joy, Florence, that thou art so great ; that over land and sea thou beatest thy wings."

From Florence to Pisa in two and a half hours, where the Leaning Tower never ceases to be an attraction, thence to Leghorn (where we called upon numerous straw-braiders but brought away little leghorn,) out through a long canal to the steamer in the Mediterranean, to try the waters which are so often called treacherous. We cannot say they have been justly so called for we slept an entire night, sailed peacefully along the borders of Italy, (so far away however that only mountain peaks appeared in sight) enjoyed a day of quiet and calm upon the blue waters, again slept and our eyes opened upon the City of Naples.

NAPLES.

Chapter XVI.

NOW we are to tell you of that "Fragment of heaven to earth vouchsafed," and more than ever we long for the poet's pen and the artist's brush, for words can hardly bring this landscape before you as the flowing musical lines of verse or the soft mellow tints in the painter's hand. We fear you will not see this grand panorama of land and sea, water and sky, bay and mountain, strait and plain, ship and fort, all bathed in melting light; nor imagine the far-away aspect, the dreamy haze, the distant liquid light. Do you see this noble Bay of Naples presenting its quiet waters to the storm-tossed ships of the Mediterranean, holding many miniature bays in its graceful curves, offering an asylum to the fleeing and the pursued on the islands which rise up like the gourd in a night and bidding defiance to invading foe by raising its forts on peak and point and manning its castles with sinew and strength — one grand curve of thirty-five miles, beautifully, gracefully divided into lesser curves! And where does this city begin or end, either in time or in space! Stretching back from all these small harbors which form the one great harbor, up to the summits which smile in perpetual summer, from point to point in almost continuous line the dwellings of man rise to view and the earth teems with life.

ILLUSTRATIONS.—1. Bay of Naples with Vesuvius in the distance. 2. Grotto of Posilippo near the summit of which is the Tomb of Virgil. 3. A Naples lond. 4. Lava bed. 5. Naples costume and employment.

With what suddenness the heavenly view vanishes from sight and how quickly a gross and disgusting and earthly one takes its place! For nearly three thousand years this city has been rising, extending and growing, varied with occasional times of falling, lessening and diminishing, changing its point of interest from one locality to another, taking one name after another according to the whim of the conqueror, marking all the eras of time by its buildings and its ruins. Only one city in our United States is its equal in population, and perhaps not one in the world is equal in the filth and squalor of its inhabitants. Imagine your rag-bags walking from their corners with their contents displayed in the most glaring manner, your " Dinah and kitchens ". set out upon the streets, and all the culinary operations performed in the sight of the world — frying, boiling, roasting, baking — the public thoroughfare a pantry and a dining-room from early dawn until the hour of midnight, — we could not take oath that it is not the sole resting place of multitudes who swarm there constantly. The little furry animal which bears most of the burdens of this country, whose hair as a general thing turns in the wrong direction if it is not all worn off his skin, and whose ears are by far the most prominent feature — this small animal provokes incessant cracks of the whip, and grunts which can only be likened to the sound one naturally makes when deprived of a tooth. Then the bugs — how can man or beast live here when the winter days are over, for the creeping creatures are very active in these coldest days of the year? Another annoyance, yes, two of them, is everywhere met in these thronged streets — the persistency of cab-drivers in trying to make everybody think that it is their duty to patronize the voitures, and the other one which we have previously mentioned — asking for alms. We have been almost near enough to Victor Emanuel to present our petition in person that he shall give the beggars a separate street in which to walk, but we let the opportunity pass, so we must see the sights of this busy, interesting ancient city with the sound of wailing in our ears and the scenes of woe before our eyes.

To readers of classical literature — Cæsar, Virgil, Cicero, Horace and Livy — on one of these mornings, when air and earth and sky all present a gilded radiance, which is transmitted to every visible object, making them seem "so near and yet so far," we go forth in the warm sunlight, to the sea, whose surges beat upon soil trod by heroes of old, and let our thoughts go out upon the sea of Time to the shades of the departed, calling up their names to people these realms if but for a passing moment. Musing, pondering, dreaming, we saunter through the streets of Neapolis, (new city) founded by the Greeks nearly three thousand years ago, and reach the portion whose foundations we may well say were laid quite three thousand years ago, so nearly that this number of years marks its age — Paleopelis, (old city) which lies from hence to the summit of Posilippo.

First and foremost among the shadowy spirits whose presence we invoked, is that of the Mantuan bard, who wrote his own epitaph in the following words: — "*Mantua me genuit, Calabri rapuere, tenet nunc Parthenope. Cecini pascua, rura, duces.*" If Virgil could make the hero of his poem descend into the infernal regions while he yet dwelt in the mortal frame, might not the poet come back to us when clothed with immortality? On these heights he once dwelt; here he wrote "Oh Muse, relate to me the causes," and here was that wonderful body laid; wonderful because it assisted the master-mind to work nineteen years before the Christian era, when the spirit soared into upper realms to try the realities of the other world. Are any of you curious to know where the dust of the immortal Virgil lies? In the part of Naples once called Parthenope, Paleopolis, Posilippo, on the side of the steep eminence Pizzafalcone, by many steps winding around among the habitations of the living and the dead in such a manner that a guide is absolutely necessary to find the spot; under a clothes-line hung with linen made yellow by washing; followed closely by beggars of all ages anxious to do something for which they may demand a few centissimi at least; until an iron gate is reached, and an old man, almost too feeble to hold his place before the eager assistants tugs at the bell with trembling hands, and when the gate is opened he enters with the favored Three as the one who has obtained admission, while the rest remain without. Curious old burying place, Roman columbarian, where the few graves are guarded to keep their places in the rocks. Down stone steps to a little storm-chamber, fifteen feet square, with three windows and a vaulted ceiling, a small tablet rises to the memory of him whose Æneid is by far his most enduring monument. We pluck a branch of delicate evergreen, which perhaps was planted by Petrarch, perhaps not, but which certainly grew by the tomb of Virgil. Paying our entrance fee and our guide, (who demands a little more for being a " bono man ") the woman who admitted us, and the old man who had haunted our footsteps, we left the burial place of the poet we so much admired in our school days, and shall continue to admire as long as sense is granted unto us.

From the tomb of Virgil we retrace our steps, and at the base of Posilippo find ourselves confronting a tall, dark opening in the mountain, which is quite in keeping with the spectral excursion we have entered upon. Bare gray rocks stare upon us as we enter the Grotto which superstition says was constructed by the wiles of the poet whose body lies within the rocks above it. With something of a shiver we step within the vaulted entrance, ninety feet in height, and with brisk steps begin the passage through the mountain. A dim light hangs upon the wall every few yards, and away in the distance we can discover a little of the light of heaven. This true light dispels the darkness of the scene, and we walk the half-mile assured that the Emperor Augustus caused this wonderful work to be performed, and that during all these eighteen centuries it has been a short way of reaching the villages on the other side of the mountain.

Again we are in the midst of crowded streets. Buildings that look as if they might have stood since the year one, and children that are almost naked enough to be angels, but without any appearance of wings, and with many signs which mark them as fallen angels, if angels they could be called. A lovely walk of four and one-half miles, on roads as hard and smooth as marble, between dark evergreens which, in our geopraphies, used to look like giant umbrellas, and which have not lost that appearance now that we look upon them rising from their native soil. Again the road skirts the seashore. This is the coast which the poems of Homer and Virgil invest with living interest; these are the realms where civilization first gained a footing on Italian soil; and here is the spot where emperors reared their villas and spent their days in luxury. But where are the princes and the palaces now? They tell us that the rocks stand upon a fiery foundation; that the earth swallows up the labor of multitudes and lifts mountains from the uncertain sea; and we contemplate these rocks with awe and wonder. Their naked sides seem to bear inscriptions made by the hand of Time, which would certainly solve the mystery if we only had the wisdom to decipher the hieroglyphics. The light of day is almost gone as we enter the gate of an old, old city, and walk through crowds which look as though they would like to devour us were it not for the warning voice of the guide at our side. Gladly we enter the one hotel, and soundly sleep the sleep of the honest, although our dreams may have been somewhat disturbed by the visions of the day and by the beating of the blue sea upon the walls of our building, creating fancies that were not all dreams of one who, although a prisoner, was greater than we, and who says, in the book of books, "And after one day the south wind blew, and we came the next day to Puteoli." This, then, was the place where Paul landed; the name only is changed a little. Is it strange, after eighteen hundred years?

Morning dawned upon Pozzuoli as rosy as though the day had not come and gone so many millions of times, and again we pursued the phantoms of the past. With a little guide who spoke in an unknown tongue, (mayhap a Mercury sent to escort the Three,) we walked in the steps of the eloquent and the learned, and saw what remains of the orator and scholar — the villa of Cicero. In imagination we heard him rehearse his orations to the waters of the deep, and fancied that they borrowed dignity and sublimity from the rolling waves. Soon Monte Nuovo appeared in sight — the mountain which was born in a single night; and so black and grim it rose over the scene that we felt that old Hercules, with shaggy brow, had stationed himself here to guard the narrow strip of land on which, it is said, he drove the bulls of Geryon across the swamp — the Via Herculea. We scarcely dared intrude upon his dominions, but we crossed with safety and came down to the borders of Lake Avernus. Down deep below the towering mountains, the summit of whose precipitous banks is shaded by the umbrageous pines, lies the fabled entrance to the infernal regions. The craters are sullen and black, and the neighboring ravines look as though they might harbor the ghostly Cimmerii which Homer mentions in his Odyssey; but we are not to be deterred from walking around the borders of the lake. Down in the depths we see ghastly forms extended; birds rise above the waters, but soon sink into the abyss below; surely this is what we used to read of the dismal Lake of Avernus! Here, too, is the very spot where the Sibyl led Æneas into the realms below. We approach the entrance to the cave of the Sibyl, but further we will not venture. Once again upon the borders of the lake, with the warm, bright sun shining upon our pathway, we examine more closely the state of affairs. Forms, not so ghastly, sit upon the stones and croak in the sunlight; birds rise over the water and settle again, because they can live upon the sea as well as upon the land; even the fair blossoms of Spring seem not to loiter in their coming, for the *taraxacum* (not *densleonis*, however) lifts its yellow head and looks very familiarly at us, one of the *campanulas* meekly rings its bell before us, and several of the *labiates* open their lips as if they could give us words of greeting; the ground everywhere is carpeted with the delicate candytuft, which grows without care or cultivation, and the variety of *papilionaceæ* which is always pleasant to the eye because it promises something sweet to the taste when the fruit in the pod shall become sufficiently mature, raises its blossoms temptingly and brings the water to our lips as we think of the time when we shall sit at the table and eat the green peas at the Fourth of July dinner with the loved ones at home. Thus were we reasoning to ourselves, when all of a sudden a loud, harsh bark sounded close to our ears, followed by one and another till we clenched our fists with very fright, and fully believed that this was the genuine Lake Avernus, and that the three-headed dog Cerberus, which guards the dark regions, had been let loose upon our track. Would he devour us? But our brave little guide rushed back with stick in hand, and at the same time a voice was heard, and when we dared to turn our heads, two monstrous hounds, as black as the regions they seemed to come from, were creeping back to their master's feet.

We will not extend our walk to the famous Bay of Baiæ, which the odes of Horace have immortalized, although the ancient temples of Minerva, Venus and Diana are seen in their fallen grandeur, and the celebrated hot baths of the infamous Nero are still at a boiling temperature, while the cruel Emperor has been cold these many centuries; nor to Cape Misino, prominent in sea and sky, although this was the point where Cæsar, Pompey and Mark Antony met to divide the Roman empire, and the point also where the fleet of Pliny was anchored when he met his cruel fate from the fires of Vesuvius; nor to Ormar, the Elysian Fields of Virgil, where he consulted the oracle before descending into Hades in search of his father's spirit, although it was here that the great Scipio breathed his last; but we will return by the spot where stand the foundations of the villa of Agrippina, in which she was destroyed by her unnatural son, Nero, back to Pozzuoli to visit the amphitheatre, noted in history, where Nero and Diocletian entered so prominently into the scenes enacted during their licentious lives, and which has lain hundreds of years buried in the lava of the neighboring volcano — buried in the oblivion which its ignominy deserves; to visit also the Temple of Jupiter Serapis, grand in its ruins as it was famous in its magnificence.

And now we will return to delightful Naples, passing the island, Nisida, where Brutus fled after the destruction of Cæsar, and where he bade farewell to his beloved Portia when he departed for the battle of Philippi, — all the way by the beautiful bay, lined with multitudes, and loaded with fruit and fish and vegetables.

In early days our imagination ran riot when we touched upon the topic of the Sea Horse, and we fancied him an immense creature, with head of horse and tail of fish, and furnished, too, with the wings of a bird, so that while his home was in the sea, he would not scorn a contest with the dwellers on land or the denizens of the air, and nothing would be free from the ravages of the monster. As we walked by the Bay of Naples we were enabled to decide how true a picture fancy had painted for us; for a ragged little Italian boy presented several specimens of the veritable Sea Horse for the foreigners to purchase. We gladly availed ourselves of the opportunity, and put into our sachel the little creature, about two inches in length, whose photograph we give our friends, together with the description of a naturalist:—

"The Sea Horse, when taken fresh from his native home, though almost laughably grotesque, is a very pretty creature. Its general color is ashen gray; at first glance, an exceedingly sober suit. But if examined more closely, it will be found thickly studded with tiny spangles of metallic silver. Add to this the rich armature of daintily carved plates, like a coat of mail, its body always partly erect, and, bent forward, it looks like the steed of a knight-errant in quest of adventure. Those pretty, golden, yet queer little eyes, chameleon-like, independent of each other, intently gaze two ways at once. Its dorsal fin is, in nature, an exquisite fan, in form, size and ornament worthy the hand of Queen Mab. As we look at his equine appearance, and think of his monkey faculty, (using his caudal extremity,) and his opossum traits, and that queer blending of innocent oddity with patriarchal dignity, we have to accept the old fisherman's proverb, 'There is nothing on the land that is not in the sea.'"

The fairest, most lovely of all the days in the year, the Indian Summer days in America, give only a faint idea of Naples, even in these mid-winter days. The first view from our window upon sea and sky told us that the weather-god was propitious, and we hastily prepared for the proposed ascent. At about the centre of this vast city a carriage took up the wandering Three and bore them along by the side of the sea, one mile after another, out through an ancient gate; still on through the busy, crowded streets, between old houses overflowing with poverty and rags: on, on, with no cessation of buildings and people, for four miles and a half, when we stopped before the office for guides and horses to ascend Vesuvius.

Arrangements were soon completed, and the Three went into the streets of Resina, (the name had changed twice, although we could not see why it was not all Naples). Two mounted, but the third still on her own footing, two men to attend to the horses, a guide for the party and two others who probably knew why they went, but we did not, constituted the company. Out through narrow lanes, between high stone walls, in places rather unfavorable for observation, in patience we threaded our

---

ILLUSTRATIONS.—1. General View of Pompeii. 2. Frescoed Wall. 3. Sea Horse. 4. Fresco, "Cave Canem."

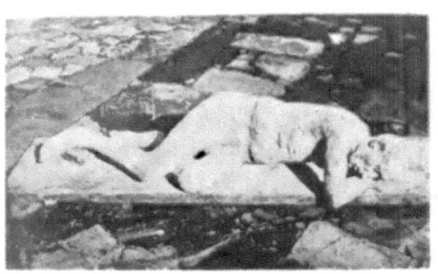

way, for we should soon be above them all. In time, we came to the lava beds of different years, spread out to view in the colors almost of the rainbow, although perhaps not quite so bright, wrought into forms which reminded us of the waves of the ocean when a brisk gale played among the waters. What a power had accomplished this wonderful work, removing all traces of everything else, burning out root and branch of nature and art, and taking possession of the entire land. In about two hours the party had reached the point where all must go upon some footing other than that of a quadruped, and it became a question whether it should be a more or less independent one. The writer will only speak for herself and charge; they went up the cone behind their guide, having no strap fastened to a man before, no hands upon the back by a man behind, no broad shoulders to bear their weight — the independent *Two* this time. One hour and a quarter among the almost perpendicular lava rocks and sand, but the climb was accomplished, the height was gained and the reward, too. But a little before we reached the highest point, we found ourselves upon smoking ground, upon ground so hot we could scarcely bear the hand upon it. Was it possible we were standing so near those restless fires, those treacherous fires which lure but to destroy? The guide said the crater had once been there; who knew where it would be next? A little farther and a year's wanderings were rewarded, the labor of many years was remunerated. We sat down and wrote at the head of a letter " Summit of Vesuvius."

On the pulverized lava, nearly black in color and sufficiently warm to sit upon, the breath of satisfaction escaped our lips while we rested from our walk, at an angle of forty-five degrees, and cast about us the glance of observation. About a yard distant on one hand, eggs were standing before a little hole in the ground, getting ready for our repast; (they brought to mind something we used to hear when children, of a fabled spot where chickens, ready roasted, went about with forks in their backs, crying "Eat me, eat me ;") about as far away, on the other hand, the gigantic mouth of the fire-god was gaping, his black, sulphurous breath casting a cloud over the head of Vesuvius, and making us feel that we were quite as near to the entrance of the infernal regions, as was Æneas on the banks of the neighboring lake of Avernus.

Eggs, beautifully cooked, were eaten, and the tour of inspection commenced. Close to the edge — not too close — we peered into the realms below; very uncertain were the objects we could distinguish, but imagination worked powerfully, aided by momentary glimpses when the smoke cleared a little, and we surely saw, on the cragged, uneven rocks, the yellow sulphur deposited in forms to vie with the corals of the deep : yellow, white, green, red, every color was there in the rocks, but the fire was too far away for our eyes to see — in that we were disappointed, although a flame was very easily produced by putting the end of a stick into the crevice where our eggs were cooked. An attempt was made to encircle this yawning mouth of the crater, to measure it with paces all unaccustomed to treading over volcanic formations, but the fumes of sulphur were overpowering.

"On all sides are gigantic serpent convolutions of black lava, their immense fold rolled into every conceivable contortion, as if, in their fiery agonies, they had struggled and wreathed and knotted together, and then grown old and black with the imperishable signs of those terrific convulsions upon them; they were flecked and streaked and dyed with the violet and pink and purple of the evening sky. Arsenic, sulphur and many a sharp and bitter salt were in everything. The sulphurous cliffs were dyed in many a brilliant shade of brown and orange by the admixture of various ores, but their brightness seemed strange and unnatural, and the dizzying whirls of vapor, now enveloping the whole scene in gloom, now lifting in this spot, now in that, seemed to magnify the dismal pit to an indefinite size."

We turned back, and soon began the descent, thankful that we had looked into the depths of Vesuvius, but more thankful that our home is not upon soil which trembles with the earthquake's shock or is liable to eruptions of red hot lava. The descent was quickly accomplished in a straight-forward direction with long strides; there was no danger of falling as there would be under ordinary circumstances, for every step planted the walker firmly in the sand, and what it had taken one and a quarters hours to *do*, was *undone* in one quarter of an hour.

At three o'clock, P. M., the riders were remounted and the return commenced. A splendid carriage road was followed and the view during the entire route was extremely fine. The sun sank into the sea seeming almost to have doubled its size and grandeur, and the new moon appeared, the ninth in number of the thirteen which we expected to wax and wane while we were wanderers in a foreign land. Nine hours had been spent, and a carriage took us back to Naples in the dark, weary enough to make our couches feel soft and good, and rest for a day somewhat desirable, especially to the riders on horseback.

At the gates of the Dead City of the Past, the shadow of the Destroyer looms up as black and as ominous as when, two thousand years ago, in the bustle and business of life, this people unconsciously prepared their own burial place. In this early spring-time, when the earthy brown is scarcely covered with garments of green, a peculiar feeling of gloom pervades the entire scene, and we sleep nervously between the half-resurrected city and the fiery mountain which holds weapons of death to hurl at the unwary who slumber at its base, and we thankfully welcome another glorious dawn which promises sunlight in the silent streets, where we will spend a day studying, musing upon the last days of Pompeii.

Through one of the eight gates we enter within the walls, which, although double, and with the intervening space filled with earth, were yet not adequate to keep out the burning, destroying foe. Intent upon our purpose, we proceed at once to the central point, the Forum, where were wont to assemble all ages and ranks, all classes and professions, to enact the busy scenes of life; we come here to draw a contrast between the past, which is partly fancied, and the present, which is entirely real, the fictitious "Days" of Bulwer, and the living times of the writer, to look with a double eye and sketch with opposite colors. Then, were coming together along the six streets which converged at this point, crowds of young and old, rich and poor, busy and idle, to spend the day in the open air, and perform the work of the time, or discuss the events of the hour, all gesticulating, gesturing after the manner of the Italians, and all unconscious of the terrible fate impending; now, after a lapse of two thousand years, to stand upon the excavated ruins of the proud Pompeii, come three *feminæ*, from the shores which were unknown until ages after this city was buried, across the broad ocean all unnavigated until Italia's son braved the scorn of the people and the storms of the deep to find the continent with its western wilds. Then, the money-changers sat in their stalls counting their coin, which were of inestimable value in their greedy eyes, but which soon would be no more than the melting minerals beneath the seething streams of lava; then, the merchants displayed their bright goods in the shops and in the streets, the itinerant cooks sold their hot morsels to the hearty and the hungry, the learned lawyers talked the Latin language, so soon to become a dead tongue to them all. Now, a few wandering and wondering women and men, with minds excited and eyes dilated, view the scene in astonishment and talk in all tongues of volcanic eruptions and recent excavations.

Within the area of the Forum were twenty-two marble pedestals proud to support the statues of the illustrious (Scipio's was prominent among the number); and unfinished pediments were in the process of completion for equestrian statues which, alas! were never to be elevated; to-day they all lie low, broken, blackened, buried, or raised only to grace the walls of some neighboring museum. In those days near the Forum stood temples to the gods and goddesses that the people worshipped with feasts and rich offerings, and appeased in their wrath with libation and blood, — Venus, Mercury, Jupiter, Fortuna and Isis; in these latter days the temples are stripped, the altars are torn down, the priests are silent and here religion is a myth.

A favorite place of resort for the Pompeians in those days of luxury was the Thermæ, fitted up in elegance; they were commodious and capacious, covering an entire square. But these baths were bathed in liquid fire, and the bathers were buried in the burning ashes.

Just at this point of ramble among the ruins, the musings of the Three were interrupted by the demands of appetite, and the question arose, where would be a suitable place to satisfy these demands. Many doors were open unto us, but we chose the house of the tragic poet, for we knew " his suppers were the best in Pompeii," and he loved literature and the fine arts, and gave his guests mental as well as bodily food. Directly opposite the baths was the home of Glaucus, the poet, and we crossed the street, which we should call narrow, certainly not wide enough for other than velocipedes to meet; the crossing was what moderns might adopt with advantage to their ladies, if not to their carriages — large, flat, high stones, with little more than space for the wheel between, lifting the walker out of the dirt and protecting her from contact with rider and steed. The road was lowered the width of these stepping stones below the pavement, and large square blocks of lava closely fitted together bear marks of the wheels in their course and prints of the hoofs. The house which we selected as the one in which to dine was small but one of the most elegant, and in other days they entered a narrow hall, where was a fierce dog in mosaic, and the words " *Cave canem.*" Nearly all the rooms were rich in paintings of the brightest hues. Classical subjects were illustrated, one of which was the admiration of all who looked upon it —

the parting of Achilles and Briseis. In the centre was a court where blossomed the most brilliant flowers in marble vases, and there was a fane dedicated to the Penates. Those who would know more of that beautiful home, that brilliant host, that sumptuous repast, must read Bulwer's description or rely upon the powers of imagination. We entered the doorway unrung and unannounced; the dog was not there even in mosaic, although other mosaics were found under the accumulated sand. "Achilles and Briseis" had gone together to the museum at Naples, but many others were still upon the walls, somewhat faded and soiled, to be sure, but beautiful nevertheless. The household gods had all departed. The Three sat down on the threshold with the walls about them, but no roof overhead, and ate their cold bread and oranges, dwelling upon the instability of earthly things.

Then through the long street of tombs — once the tombs of the dead, afterwards the tombs of the living, to the house of Diomed. Here wealth was manifest in everything; the cellars were stocked with wine to grow old. The purse was filled with gold to save, and the key was in the hands of the servant to keep foe from the treasures. But alas! the wine is too old in the casks, the hand that carried the purse is colder than the gold, the key and the servant are useless; the seventeen who had fled to the cellar from the eruption of the volcano, made an impression so lasting upon the walls and the rocks, that after two thousand years we can tell much concerning their fate.

Six hours we have walked in this city so suddenly quieted in its activity and life, so long buried from the sight of the world, and we feel how wise it is that we know not what our end will be, nor in what day or hour it will come. The Past is open and full of instruction in regard to the deeds of the Present, but the Future must continue to be a sealed volume to all.

Our walk is not finished yet. Just across the fields of lava, fields already commencing the labor of the year, still at the base of the dread mountain we see the village of Castellamare rising from the ashes of Stabia, which shared one and the same fate with Pompeii. This was the spot where Pliny, leaving his fleet across the bay, came to witness the phenomenon of a mountain on fire, but he was unable to flee himself, and he died the victim of philosophical research and kindly love for his fellow creatures. On, by the side of the sea, with the bold bare mountains at our left, and the bright blue bay at our right, through a most picturesque village cut in two by a deep, cragged defile running from the sea back into the heart of the hills — the Vicus Equinus of the ancients — we merely continue the course previously described and double the bright pictures we looked upon then, over the famous route which everybody takes to the beautiful plain of Sorrento, for miles through olive orchards and orange groves, crossing the wildest ravines, whose depths are covered with lemon trees, the bright green beautifully sprinkled with the yellow fruit; and whose rocky sides are trained to nurture the vine and fig tree; through this scene of loveliness, nineteen miles from Naples and just across the bay, the birth-place of Tasso is reached. It is not strange that such eloquence and poetry have emanated from these regions. Stand in the poet's birthplace and listen to the roll of the waves, the whirl of the waters and the wail of the winds; see the sudden squall on this stormy sea chase the sunshine from shore to shore, raising the feathery billows in pretended wrath till the breast of the deep seems covered with birds of snowy plumage; then you will appreciate the lessons the sea gives to her sons. Sorrento, the loveliest of the lovely, adds to the little treasures of these sachels and shawl-straps some showy silken scarfs and wood work, wrought in wonderful ways, and we add the name of Sorrento to the list of delightful days spent in this terrestrial paradise.

But now we can vouch for the fickleness of the Mediterranean. With the pleasure of a walk around the beautiful Bay of Naples, (about thirty of the fifty-three miles we had already passed,) we had connected the idea of a visit to the island of Capri and its grotto, so gorgeously grand that we might imagine that Tiberius, whose house was long amid its beauties, had prepared the place for his infamous orgies. The rays of light reach this cave in the sea only through the waters which rob them of all their colors except the azure, hence its sides are a heavenly blue and it takes the name of Azure Grotto.

The waves rolled high and beat upon the rocks, and the winds rolled too around the jagged peaks so that not a mortal dared man a boat and trust himself on the uneasy deep. In spite of the winds we went over the ground where "Agnes of Sorrento" walked with her grandmother, entering the orange groves and plucking the golden fruit which our hands could easily reach, by the side of the pale green olive terracing the mountain sides, over the deep defiles which the angry sea has cut for itself— four miles toward Massa where we might be nearer to Capri. Entering the limits of this town more dead than Pompeii, we asked for a hotel. A bright boy left his horse standing in the middle of the street and with a cunning look over his shoulder kept saying, "Come along, come along!" We tried to talk with him but he only replied "Come along, come along!" Passing through streets narrower than the closes of Edinboro, he knocked loudly at a gate which after a time was opened and we were conducted to the one room we conclude, where were a number of beds for the weary to rest, but scarcely another article of furniture in sight. We concluded to return to the Hotel Tasso, and the next day went back to the city born of a sea nymph. A little longer with these idle inhabitants, a few more days under these sunny skies, and hand in hand with youthful Spring, we turn our course toward more northern regions. We trust the fair goddess will not desert us, but will strew our pathway with blossoms many, and deck the garlands above our heads as we seek again the land of our birth.

Adieu, fair Napoli! May your skies be ever golden, your waters sparkle in the bright sunlight, your mountains and Islands be crowned with roseate hues, and may Vesuvius nurse the fires within his own burning breast, and the earthquakes leave you undisturbed. Naples, farewell!

ROME.

Chapter XVII.

A NIGHT'S ride through the Campagna of Italy, and early morning opened our eyes upon Rome. Rome! — Rome! — Regal Rome! Seven weeks within her walls and among her seven hills — weeks which had their days doubled, their hours heaped up, their minutes multiplied, yea, their seconds stretched out almost into centuries — and the wandering Three were so burdened, oppressed, weighed down by the accumulation of time, the passing away of generations, the changes in form of government, that their hands refused to do their bidding, the ink dried upon the pen, the mind lost itself in the maze of thought, and letters were unwritten because there was so much to say.

Rome is not like any other city. It is the city of all cities; it represents the time of all times; it is in very truth the Eternal City. Up and down her seven hills, round about her massive walls, along beside the yellow Tiber, slowly under the famous arches, toiling up the crumbling towers, delving deep in the buried ruins, gazing with wonder at the works of art, — was it strange that, like Rip Van Winkle, we knew not ourselves?

ILLUSTRATIONS.—1. Romulus and Remus nursing the wolf. 2. General view of Rome, entering at the Porta del Popolo (Gate of the People). 3. Obelisk brought from Egypt, in centre of Piazza del Popolo. 4. The street called the Corso, passing between the Twin Churches, Via Ripetta at the right, Via Babuina at the left. 5. The Capitol, a little beyond the Corso, on the Capitoline Hill, the Colosseum at the left. 6. The Tiber, passing through the city, with the Castle of St. Angelo, the Piazza St. Peter, the Cathedral and Vatican on the right.

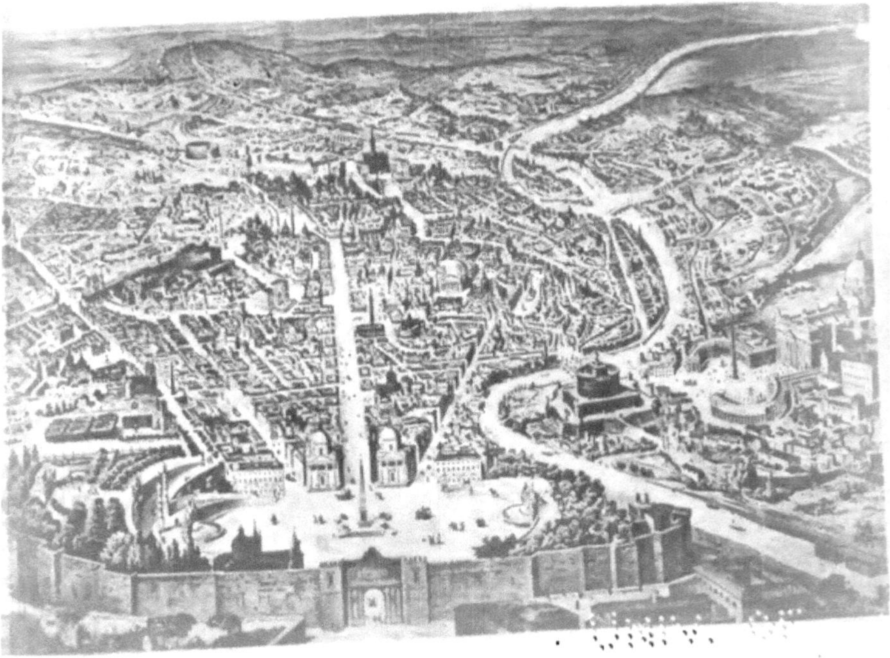

We stand upon the Aventine, and again we live the early days of that other life when all the world was forgotten, and, infatuated, we followed the Dardanian chief, the "goddess-born Æneas," fleeing from conquered Troy to where —

> "In the shady shelter of a wood,
> And near the margin of a gentle flood,
> He beheld a sow upon the ground,
> With thirty sucking young encompassed round."

We see the Trojans leave the main and enter the wood,

> "Which thick with shades and a brown horror stood,"

and soon we see the hundred ambassadors, laden with presents, on their way to King Latinus, who receives them within his portico of a hundred columns, standing on this same Mount Aventinus, accepts the sceptre of old Priam, and sends a gift of three hundred horses and a chariot for the pious Æneas. Near the base of this mountain stood the fig tree (*ficus ruminalis*) where

> "By the wolf were laid the martial twins,"

and at its summit, in after years, Remus stood while his brother Romulus was stationed upon Palatinus to watch the flight of birds and take the auguries to decide who should found the city about to be built. To-day we cross this lowest of the seven hills, we pass from base to opposite base, and what do you think we see? A beautiful blue sky overhead, but almost nothing else; for the narrow, dusty streets are shut in by smooth, high brick walls, which allow not a glimpse of the great green vineyards behind them; and were we taking auguries, the birds must fly high or we should not read aright. We muse and dream, and say within ourselves, Truly the world has changed within twenty-five hundred years.

Down toward the setting sun we turn our steps and seek the muddy river, which has wound its way to the sea regardless of the flight of time or deeds of men, to the point where the Pons Sublicius, oldest of the bridges across the Tiber, was immortalized by the brave defense of Horatius Cocles, standing alone on its tottering timbers till all support was cut away, then with his heavy armor on he swam to the shore, leaving the enemy looking wistfully across. This scene brings back an oration to which we often listened with thrilling interest from a bright-eyed youth of wondrous powers, and so it brings back Cortland Academy and the village green, happy hours and pleasant scenes, childhood and home. But the bridge which the brave Horatius "kept so well" has followed him into the waves of the Tiber, and, like him, been swallowed up by the waves of Time. No bridge and no Horatius Cocles!

To the north of the mountain we have described, (deserted and old, still fertile and fresh,) rises another of the seven hills, the Capitoline, with its saddle-backed ridge crowned with two peaks, Ara Cœli and Monte Caprino, and the intervening space known as Intermontane. Oh, for words and time to tell what this mountain has borne and these peaks have seen! Strabo and Livy have told us that nature once adorned these summits with trees, and that in the intervening space between these two groves Romulus, the first king of Rome, opened an asylum for those fleeing from justice, and brought together assassins and outcasts from all lands, and so furnished citizens for his new city. Then where could wives be found for such a set of men? But the carrying off of the Sabine women belongs to another part of Rome. Wives were stolen, and the inhabitants increased and multiplied under the king whose nurse was a wolf and whose subjects were monsters of wickedness. On the eastern point of the Capitoline mount, called Ara Cœli, (Altar of Heaven,) they reared a temple to Jupiter, which stood for centuries and furnished a place of worship for these godless creatures to satisfy the spark of conscience still burning within their breasts. It did something else too — it gave us the name of Capitol; for in digging for the foundations of this temple the head was found of a man named Tolus, (caput Toli,) so the building was called Capitol, and the name has since been given to head buildings in other lands.

But pause, my pen, and cease your scribbling; for vain is the effort to enumerate the smallest part of the daring deeds and wondrous works of mighty men and numerous hosts all along down from Romulus to Victor Emanuel. What crowns Mons Capitolinus to-day? Our eyes open wide with wonder, our feet hasten on with alacrity, we approach the spot where the ages are heaped in a mingled mass. High, high up the six score steps, on the point toward the rising sun, appropriately stands the Church of Ara Cœli, upon that Altar of Heaven which once bore the heathen temple to Jupiter Capitolinus. Here, as was most fit, in this church so high, near the spot where Rome took its rise, Gibbon conceived the idea of describing the Decline and Fall of the Roman Empire.

A few steps downward and we stand in the Piazza del Campidoglio and face the Senatorial Palace which rises from the ancient Tabularium which in its turn rises from something older beneath it, (this massive foundation was once the receptacle of the archives of republican Rome, and communicated with the grand old Forum at its base, both of which have for centuries lain under the soil). A palace at our right and a palace at our left, both full of mementoes of the past which we could have spent the weeks in examining. There sit in cold silence the marble images of many who have added to the long history of this old city, famous and infamous, cruel and kind, patrician and plebeian in impressive array, surrounded by the fruits of their labors corroded and defaced by the hand of time.

Ye social readers of "The Marble Faun," under the guidance of Hawthorne and one of the "Independent Three," imagine yourselves in the capitol at Rome. In the center of the first room we have entered after ascending the stairs the Gladiator is still dying; Juno, Apollo, the Antinous and the Amazon all stand the same cold, unmoved observers of his agony, and the Faun of Praxiteles smiles on the scene, sad as it is, — the Faun, combining in one and the same form marks of the human and the animal natures, the impress of mind and the pointed, leaf-shaped ears of the lower animals — the Marble Faun, which was for hundreds of years buried under the ruins of the past, then raised again to be placed as a gem of the sculptor's art in this modern museum on the old Capitoline Hill, and to become the theme of a most beautifully told tale of a well-known American writer.

We look from one of the windows of this famous Capitoline museum down upon the buildings, some of which saw the dawn of Christianity, over the arch of Septimus Severus, not so triumphal as in the days of its erection; the Roman Forum, name reiterated in all ages as the era of Roman power, lying in the valley between the Capitoline and Palatine mounts; on to the Coliseum, the grandest of colossal ruins; — over all this we looked as did the former imaginary personages in the story to which we have alluded; and we too were pressed down with weighty reminiscences, our lives were swallowed up in the grand events transacted within the small space coming within our vision. With one of the four, we felt that the Gladiator is too long in the very act of death, and we left him to walk with the four in their romantic wanderings through the city of the Cæsars, this capital of the world. Through one hall after another, gazing upon antique sculpture of dead heroes and rulers, mythical gods and goddesses, imaginary Fauns and Satyrs, warlike Minervas and lovely Venuses, powerful Hercules and terrible Jupiters, until the eqilibrium of our brain seemed very much disturbed, and we could easily imagine all joining in a sylvan dance with the frisky Faun as their leader.

The brazen wolf which centuries ago gave the unnatural supply to the deserted boys in the Roman Forum is religiously preserved for coming generations to see, and still supplies models for pictures and casts which are everywhere seen in the streets of Rome. In the center of the piazza, the noble horse of Marcus Aurelius still prances and paws as he did in the days when the prince of sculptors, Michael Angelo, said, "See, he moves," and the first and seventh mile stone stand almost side by side up here, so long has been the time since they measured the weary way on the Via Appia to Paul going forth to death. Constantine and his son are prominent here as they are in the annals of the church and crown, and Castor and Pollux stand by the side of their colossal steeds and guard the steps to this famous mount. Can you not see this one of the seven hills with the ruins at its base, the relics on its face, and the church and capitol crowning its summit?

Perhaps our friends for the sake of variety would take a long stride from the hill-tops of Rome to the valleys between, from the dead images of the past to the living forms of the present, from the dome of the Capitol to the Corso Victor Emanuel. They will surely feel that they have leaped over the ages, over time and space, and have been suddenly transported into fairy realms. The windows are brilliant with shining pearls and pictured mosaics, with varied marble and cunningly wrought bronze, with portraits that speak and statues that breathe, with the colors of the rainbow and the skill of inspiration. Balconies have been builded from story to story, bordered with crimson and colors bright, crowded with people far and near. The streets are dense with the crowds that gaze, they are alive with the numbers that throng their midst, they are wild with the tumult that comes from the many, they are fantastic with the costumes that cover the multitudes, they are strange with the masks that hide the true-face, they are comical with the mixture of nature and race. For what has the world come together in Rome? It is the grand carnival time and now all labor, and care, and thought are given to the winds and melted into air; the old have become young again, the hideous have become beautiful, the sirens have become dancing fauns, and the tarantala is gaily performed to the music of tambourines. For days the Corso is the scene of confusion and everybody is pelted with flowers and confetti, and then the world goes back to its duties and the Three return to their wandering ways.

Most interesting of the forty-six Piazzas (public squares) of this ancient city is the Piazza di San Pietro, which we cross the Ponte St. Angelo to visit, and standing in front of the most magnificent modern monument in the world, the Basilica di St. Pietro. We gaze upon this grand elliptical amphitheatre surrounded by a semi-circular portico formed of 284 columns in four rows, and this surmounted by 140 colossal statues. In the centre stands the Egyptian obelisk, 72 feet high, which Caligula brought to Rome and placed in the circus of Nero, for it is here that the most despicable of despots sent his name in infamy down to coming generations by the massacre of the Christians. At each side of this church, which is the largest in the world, are the equestrian statues of Constantine and Charlemagne, which send the mind galloping back through the ages of the past to the year 326, when Constantine commenced the construction of a basilica, and carried with his own hands twelve baskets of earth in honor of the twelve apostles. After a thousand years this gave place to the present grand structure, the wonder of the world. It occupied 178 years in building and 350 to perfect it; cost $50,000,000, and covers eight acres; 54,000 persons can be accommodated at a time within its walls. It contains 290 windows, 748 columns, 47 altars, and 380 statues. Two of the master minds which the world has ever produced devoted their best years to the construction of this building, and the genius and skill of Raphael and Michael Angelo are seen in all its parts. On the summit of the facade, 149 by 370 feet, are the statues of Christ and the twelve apostles. We enter one of the five doors which give access to the vestibule and stand and wonder and gaze through the long central nave 89 feet broad, 152 feet high, to the tribune 607 feet away in the distance; past the eight fluted Corinthian pilasters, each a house of

---

ILLUSTRATIONS.—1. Piazza of St. Peter with its obelisk in the center. 2. Cathedral of St. Peter and the Vatican. 3. Interior of St. Peter. 4. Statue of St. Peter. 5. Sistine Chapel in the Vatican, with M. Angelo's Last Judgment. 6. Statue of Laocoon.

Piazza di S. Pietro.

Interno della Basilica
di S. Pietro.

Cappella Sixtina.

itself; past the eight chapels each a church of itself where divine service is performed, and you know it not until you are close upon it; past the bronze statue of St. Peter, black as Jupiter Tonans, whom it is said by some to represent, and whose great toe is polished by the kisses of the faithful; past the beautiful bronze canopy supported by four spiral columns under which is the high altar where the pope only celebrates mass (and still beneath is said to be the tomb of St. Peter, although many think there is no evidence that he ever saw the city of Rome); still farther along we come under the beautiful dome designed by Michael Angelo which lets the broad light of heaven in upon the four evangelists so high above us that the pen in the hands of one, although seven feet in length, seems of but common size. But we came in with the curious to ascend to the dome of this cathedral. Many had gone before us for the doors were open from eight to eleven, and probably hundreds came after us as we learned at the end. The minutes went by and yet we kept stepping up stair after stair, ascending flight after flight arranged in every conceivable way, on and still on to the heights above. We never before attempted to walk through the mazes of a labyrinth but now we had entered upon a route which seemed endless. "The roof seems of itself a little city — covered towers, cottages, cisterns, plains and hills, slopes and precipices." One of our number gave out again and stopped midway between earth and the cross-crowned summit, while the two passed on together for the highest point. The space through which we walked grew narrow and the constantly increasing numbers crowded compactly together, each pushing and striving to enter before his neighbor; the tall burly men almost crushed the American Coon climbing to heights where coons seldom go. At last, with the sixteen who alone could enter the bronze ball at the same time, we passed through the door which was closed and fastened by the guard; again we mounted an almost perpendicular flight of stairs, where the last flight rose entirely perpendicular, a ladder in fact, which we ascended, and while our backs pressed against the opposite wall our faces almost touched the wall in front. Where were we? In the dome of St. Peter with only the cross above us of the 146 feet from the pavement below. Sixteen crouching figures, for we could by no means stand erect, moving around in a brass ball, stopping every step or two to put an eye to the minute openings which looked out upon the country of the Tiber, and down into the old streets where men looked like specks in the sands of time; peering out toward the sea sixteen miles away, our vision of Ænas and the Trojans suddenly vanished, dissipated by a harsh voice bidding us descend and give place to others. About four hours (it occupied) to go to the summit of St. Peter, and it was a laborious work but one which we have never regretted.

From the Basilica de San Pietro in Vaticano to the Palazzo del Vaticano it is but a few steps, and we ascend the Scala Regia, with the equestrian statue of Constantine guarding the base and the less lifeless guards moving up and down in picturesque Swiss costume, the dress adopted in the time of Michael Angelo and worn to the present day. The date of the building of this largest palace in the world, (1300 by 1000 feet,) this home of the Popes, is said to be unknown; but it existed in the time of Charlemagne, for he occupied it when he visited Rome, in the year 800, to be crowned by Leo III. Modesty bids us bow our heads and speak few words as we walk day after day through the halls and galleries and museums of this famous edifice, where we seem to tread on holy ground and breathe an atmosphere almost divine. Through the Sistine Chapel — so called from Sixtus IV., who ordered its erection — ornamented with the finest works of Michael Angelo; the paintings on the ceiling, which occupied him twenty-two months, representing the Creation, the Fall of Man and the Deluge; his most celebrated painting, the Last Judgment, covers the entire end of the chapel, thirteen feet in

Univ. of
California

breadth, and occupied his fruitful mind and skillful hand almost seven entire years; while the paintings on the side walls represent the life of Mary and the life of Christ. Through the Loggia of Raphael, terminating the royal staircase, and consisting of three tiers of most beautiful porticoes surrounding an open court, where "Raphael's Bible" is laid before the beholder in fifty-two pictures on the vaults of the arches, representing facts from the Old Testament; the one over the entrance, of the Eternal Father, was executed by Raphael's own hand, the remainder were designed by him and executed by his pupils. Through the gallery of pictures, where, among the choice collection, is the Transfiguration on Mount Tabor, wet with the colors of the artist when, only thirty-two years of age, the Angel of Death transported him to regions where, we trust, he paints with heavenly dyes, — fit production of the illustrious master to lead the funeral procession to his tomb in the Pantheon, and to occupy henceforth its position at the head of all paintings, fresh throughout the ages. Through the Stanze of Raphael, consisting of four halls which, it is said, have not their equal in the world in extent, composition, color, and general execution; one, called the Hall of Constantine, representing incidents in the life of that emperor — his baptism, the appearance of the fiery cross, and his victory over Maxentius. Through the various museums, where everything old and curious is seen, with the Torso Belvidere, fragment of a statue of Hercules, and the celebrated group of Laocoon, a statue dug up with the seventy thousand about Rome which come from the ages of the past, taking us back to the days of Virgil, when we read that the serpents, "*ardentes oculos suffecti sanguini et igni*," destroyed Laocoon and his two sons, — days when the wooden horse was brought into Troy; a statue which is a remnant of Greek sculpture, carried to Paris in 1797 by Napoleon, and returned when his reign was finished.

ILLUSTRATIONS.—1. Raphael. 2. The Transfiguration. 3. The Sistine Madonna. 4. St. Cecelia in Ecstacies.

We would linger long, but must needs break away, for we have seen but a small part of the Eternal City. We might go out through a subterranean passage by which the Pope escaped when Rome was sacked in the sixteenth century, and took refuge in the castle which we find at the other extremity. This castle or fort, which has many times seen bloody service, was raised for an entirely different purpose and one far more peaceful — as a tomb for the Emperor Hadrian and his family and successors. It is said to have been covered with marble and adorned with colossal groups of men and horses, the statue of Hadrian crowning the whole. But War regards not the sacred resting-place of the dead nor the beautiful creations of the artist or sculptor, and in 537, when the Goths besieged the Greeks here, the beautiful statues were hurled down upon the besiegers and trampled under foot of man and beast. Now it is a castle instead of a mausoleum, and bears the name of St. Angelo, from the bronze statue of St. Michael, the archangel, which rises from the summit. Walking through this interesting fort down into the dismal dungeon where Beatrice Cenci (Beatreechy Chenchy the Italians call her,) wept away the weary weeks, we understood why one sad face looks down upon us everywhere in Rome. We seemed to see the sad face of this maiden so young, as it was painted by the artist within her prison walls in the Castle of St. Angelo the evening before her execution — the sorrowful face which looks out from so many of the windows of Rome, with great beseeching eyes of brown that tell their tale of weeping and of woe; that face which is radiant in its turban of white, and which haunts the observer from palace to garret; the same face, the original of which, fresh from the artist's hand, looked upon us from the walls of the Barberini Palace, now like a spectre seemed to look down from the grim walls of the old nameless palace and repeat its story of patricide (almost justifiable) and execution upon the block.

ILLUSTRATIONS.—1. Castle of St. Angelo. 2. Beatrice Cenci. 3. Hilda's Tower. 4. Fountain of Trevi.

As we entered the large, bare room where, our guide informed us, her trial was conducted, we saw at the farther extremity a half-opened door and a face peering intently upon us. We walked quietly and spoke low as we were led in that direction, but what was our astonishment to find it was only a portrait on the wall — the portrait of Beatrice's Judge, who, listening breathlessly to the testimony of the witnesses, was sketched by the artist, and lives with the prisoner and painter — Beatrice Cenci and Guido Reni. We walked between the statues of the twelve Apostles out over the bridge of many a century, the Ponte St. Angelo.

One sunny day in February we three walked forth to see — we knew not what, only something to wonder at. Of a sudden we stopped. Was it? Yes, it must be — Hilda's Tower! "Square, massive, lofty, battlemented," with the Virgin's shrine and the image before which the light has been burning many centuries. Hawthorne could not pause in his story to tell you the legend connected with this shrine; we give you merely the outlines. In the days when Rome was younger and her palaces were newer, the lord and lady who dwelt in elegance here left their babe, which was as dear as all babies are to the hearts which beat for them, in the care of a faithful servant. The watchful nurse placed the babe on the floor and stepped in, as was natural, to sympathize with one of kindred employment. When the visit was ended the child was gone — where! oh, where! The frantic woman sought everywhere, and finally learned that a mischievous monkey had undertaken the care of the forsaken little one, and had borne it to the highest point of this palatial residence. Crazy with fear, she prostrated herself and made vows which moved the heart of the Virgin to save the beloved child. The delighted parents raised this shrine, and this is the light which Hilda is represented as tending so faithfully, and this the dovecote where the American artist girl dwelt among the doves.

As we stood there in the dirty streets, and looked wishfully up to the rays so high, a vision flitted past, in form like a dove, pure and white as an angel. We can never tell whether it was imagination, or one of Hilda's doves come down to greet the three sisters from the American shores. Through the portal of this palace, over the hard, dirty stone pavement, through the dingy, dark halls, and up the stone steps rising story after story, where in different ages prince and peasant, beggar and artist have turned their course, went the wandering Three to call at the door of the Dovecote, where the copyist entered on her mission to the Virgin's shrine; and within which, drawing upon her memory, she copied so correctly the mournful, beautiful Beatrice Cenci from the original of the renowned Guido Reni. Beatrice Cenci is one of the characters too numerous to mention, whose names are indelibly written in the records of history — Roman history — and Hilda the Dove will henceforth hold a place among the fictitious characters which have so particularly interested all readers in the true and living ones.

The moon rode through the cloudless sky, casting shadows in the Eternal City, creating images in the sparkling fountains, looking shyly round the corners where centuries have gone into darkness, peeping over the massive buildings reared by the hand of ancient lords, and through the dim halls of once georgeous palaces, lighting up the tall obelisk that once stood upon the Nile, and making the hieroglyphics tell wondrous tales, pouring into the Golden House, which Nero raised for his statues and paintings and frescoes and mosaics, and most of all his cruel self, and into the baths which Titus built over the wealth of his notorious predecessor; glancing at the fallen columns which once stood in the crowded Forums, but now lie broken in the dust below; climbing to the heights of the abode of the Cæsars, and picturing with golden fingers the royal mag-

---

ILLUSTRATIONS.—1. Capitoline Mount with the equestrian statue of Marcus Aurelius in the center of the Piazza Campidoglia, Church of Ara Cœli at the right, the Capitol at the left; Castor and Pollux by the side of their steeds guarding the steps. 2. The Coliseum by Moonlight. 3. Arch of Constantine and Arch of Titus. 4. Roman Forum. 5. Back of the Capitol.

nificence in this home of the Emperors, yea, looking back to the home of the kings who ruled and reigned in this city of fabulous origin on the peak of the Palatine, and gleaming upon the walls of that wonder of the world — the Coliseum.

Coming from the hall of a Roman house which needs not the light of waxen tapers, the Three went forth with their company doubled and walked through the streets as did the artists and sculptors on their moonlight ramble, coming out too upon the same piazza where the waters have played in their virgin purity ever since the Aqua Virgo was pointed out a thirsty soldier by a maiden of charms, fourteen miles from the busy city, and brought underground more than a score of years before the Christian era to adorn this spot in the midst of active life. For nineteen hundred years Neptune has stood above these waters on a stupendous shell and Tritons have guided his sea-horses, while health and fertility have dispensed blessings in the flowing water of the fountain of Trevi. We stood upon the borders of this fountain, with the music of the waters sounding in our ears, and the play of the moonlight before our eyes, and again fancy took possession of us, and we sailed over the waters of this miniature lake with sea-nymphs at our side and the Faun upon the shore. We were not ready to drink of this fountain, but the eve before we left Rome, we stood upon the borders and quaffed the water that will ensure our return.

On we went to the Forum of Trajan, which excels all the other forums in magnificence of marble and splendor of sculpture, where stands the grand column with its records in stone of the deeds of the emperor among the Dacians, and where lies on the verge of the space hollowed out, the gray, granite column so vast in its fallen grandeur that we can scarcely imagine the force that could have raised it or the ruin of its fall. Being in an altogether mythical mood, we called, "Trajan! Trajan!" and fancied his spirit coming down in the moonlight and standing with Peter on the summit of the column, and we left him to look over the change which centuries had wrought, while we passed on by the ruins of three temples to as many gods and goddesses, on to the Coliseum.

The Coliseum by moonlight. The great black ruin is none too large to bear the inscriptions of death and destruction, of toil and torture, of woe and wretchedness — none too vast to give the names and numbers of men and hearts whose blood was here shed for the gratification of the populace — none too black to tell the story ; — and the moonlight was none too bright to bring out the weird ghosts of the eighty thousand who sat on these seats with Vespasian at their head and grinned with savage delight at the horrible scenes enacted below. Nature has tried to hide this monument so monstrous, has sprinkled it with sands that lie thick upon its breast, but man will not permit that it shall be buried with forgetfulness ; he digs away the accumulated dirt, delves to the foundation, and we looked upon the sad story written in letters of light. The Coliseum by moonlight! Who would not cross the broad Atlantic to look upon its massive walls?

> "A ruin — yet what ruin! from its mass
>   Walls, palaces, half cities have been reared ;
>   Yet oft the enormous skeleton ye pass,
>   And marvel where the spoil could have appeared.
>   Hath it indeed been plundered or but cleared ?
>   It will not bear the brightness of the day,
>   Which streams too much on all years, man, have reft away.
>
> But when the rising moon begins to climb
>   Its topmost arch, and gently pauses there ;
> When the stars twinkle through the loops of time,
>   And the low night breeze waves along the air,
> The garland forest, which the gray walls wear,
>   Like laurels on the bald first Cæsar's head ;
> When the light shines serene but doth not glare,
>   Then in this magic circle raise the dead,
> Heroes have trod this spot, 'tis on their dust ye tread."

May the hand of memory not be treacherous in delineation that we may always have this picture before us.

Out from the arches of the old amphitheatre upon the old Roman pavement on whose broad flat stones Cicero marked the dignity of his orations, and Horace measured the rhythm of his verse, perhaps upon the very one colored by the blood of the pure Virginia who was sacrificed by her father to be saved from slavery, along the Via Sacra, where the sacrifices of Romulus were offered, by the site of temples in their ruined grandeur, under the triumphal arch erected to Titus when he had conquered Jerusalem and brought the Jews here as captives, by those columns looking weird in the broad sunlight and in the dim moonlight spectral and ghastly, we walked over the space which is narrow in steps but broad beyond measure in important events, the space where history has exhausted herself and lain down to rest between the hills so celebrated, the Palatine and the Capitoline, the space most famous in ancient Rome — the Roman Forum. Here trod the man who was once nursed by a wolf, here lived the man who laid the foundation of Rome's greatness; and Rome to-day feeds and nourishes, in a cage by her public buildings, the wolf, as the preserver of her founder.

Another day when the first pink blossoms had appeared on the almond tree, we walked through the garden gate that keeps the curious from the Tarpeian Rock without the payment of a few soldis, and stood upon the spot which was always a place of great interest; it was here that the woman was covered with shields because the soldiers bore them in their left hands, and that was what they had promised to her if she would open the gate of the city unto them, (she meant their rings and bracelets.) False men! We bent over the parapet and imagined the sensation of being hurled to the base — the traitors of old and the Capuchin of the Forum by the Faun.

Many times we entered the Church of the Capuchins, standing a little off the Piazza Barberini, and a monk with the brown frock and cowl drew the curtain from before Guido's Archangel, and we remembered the criticisms of the heroine of our tale that the Archangel is too feminine and fair and gentle. We went with this monk to the basement, through four chapels opening one into the other, all decorated in a most uncommon manner with the different bones of the human body, put together in ways to represent flowers, and trees, and bouquets in baskets, and wreaths and various things which are ordinarily pleasant to look upon, but here ghastly and terrible. In the little space of ground within each chapel is soil brought from Jerusalem, in which twelve can be buried at a time, and when a monk of this order dies, the one who has lain longest in the holy ground is taken up to give place to his brother, and his bones are taken to ornament the walls. In several instances the body is in such a state of preservation that it is placed entire in some nook or corner, and there grins ever at the living and the dead. Four thousand bodies have lain in this holy earth; but no more will lie there, for Victor Emanuel has forbidden to bury within the city. Within this church, in the dim light, we fancied the dead monk lying in brown frock and cowl with beads and crucifix hanging from his girdle, just as he had been thrown from the Tarpeian Rock, and the mournful burial chant sounded in our ears, and we shivered with the heroes of "Marble Faun," who looked upon the work which their hands had wrought.

The Bambino is one of the sights of Rome and we will describe it in the words of another: "The Bambino is a wooden figure made to represent the infant Jesus. We are assured that it was made from a tree of the Mount of Olives and carved by St. Luke. It is carefully preserved in a casket of wood. Its dress is of the finest fabrics trimmed with lace and covered with jewels. Better in the eyes of the faithful than hydropathy, homeopathy, or allopathy is Bambinopathy. In times of dire distress it is taken from its chapel in the church Ara Cœli and carried to

---

ILLUSTRATIONS.—1. Capuchin Monk. 2. Burial place of the Capuchins. 3. Beggar Boy. 4. Bambino.

visit the sick, who either die or get well. Michael Angelo's Moses is the piece of statuary which if marble could speak would tell us tales of interest, but it looks coldly and quietly upon all transactions within the church St. Pietro in Vinculis.

On a lovely bright day, one of the first of February, having finished one of those penitential pilgrimages our author tells us about, over the little lava stones, pointed all so as to give an uneasy feeling to the walker's feet, we passed through the Porto del Popolo, in company with the so-called Faun, to visit the suburban Villa Borghese. A few feet from the old, old walls, a few paces from the grim old gate, (interesting, however, because we knew that the greatest of architects made the design,) the sylvan spirit takes possession of us, and we gaily dance along the graveled walks under the graceful boughs of the ilex-trees, bowing and bending and extending their branches until they form a continued green covering above our heads ; by the prim poplars and the shady cypress ; over the starry and pink-petaled daisies, the pretty purple anemones, and the golden-yellow blossoms which nearly carpet the ground. Is it strange that in the midst of this sylvan scene we fancied the Faun with his furry ears, and the Nymph with his sunny smile, dancing in delight through the glassy glades ; and, when the delightful day drew to an end and we went back to the walls of ancient Rome, — is it strange that we felt we had spent a day in romance and in fable ?

Again, when February was just bidding adieu to her consort Spring, the visit was repeated to this same Borghese Villa — this same sylvan grove — and returning with hands laden with bright blossoms, we took a stroll on the Pincian. Up from the Piazza del Popolo, from the very foot of that old red obelisk, which is one of the eleven these roaming Romans have brought from the Nile and left but eight to cast their long shadows there; up by the smooth, hard road, which makes many acute angles in its course, to the proud peak of the Pincian ; up to that point which overlooks that bit of the oldest, old wall, (hardly the one that Remus leapt over, however, for methinks it is rather too high for that,) the Muro Torto ; and, standing with faces toward the dim, distant Soracti, looking over the Campagna lying without the walls, a visionary Faun walked through the Flaminian Gate, soon followed by those other fictitious characters so closely connected with our tale. We went slowly beside the parapet, winding our way among the crowds of people speaking in almost every language but Italian, in the midst of carriages bearing many who like ourselves came from the far Western wilds, by the side of amusements which recalled the gay Champs Elysées and brought together all ages and ranks ; we looked upon Rome, the Rome of all time. We saw St. Peter's, the church of the world, over which the spirit of Michael Angelo seems to hover; we saw the round Pantheon with the relics of Raphael, whose single eye looks constantly heavenward ; we saw — we saw — we saw all this city which has stood so long that it has become its own sepulchre, which has covered and dug up its own bones, which has burned and resurrected its offspring. We looked upon the evening sunset, we listened to the vesper bells, and from the summit of the oft ascended steps, from the Piazza di Spagna, we went down the Via Sistina, and near the Fountain of the Triton refreshed tired nature with food and drink requisite for the occasion.

NORTHERN ITALY.

Chapter XVIII.

ROME has become a vision of the past, gone with her walls and her hills and her ruins and her Tiber into the storehouse of memory, with Naples and her dreamy bay, with Venice and her funereal gondolas, with all Italy and her sunny views. In the light of the twinkling stars we drank our *au revoir* from the waters of Trevi, and slept one more night in the city where seven weeks had passed as a day. Then began our course from Italy to England, from Rome to London, from the Tiber to the Thames, from the Mediterranean to the Atlantic, and with fair Spring everywhere greeting us, we were homeward bound.

A day's ride of but little interest, through a country which looked as though it had delivered up its wealth in ages long gone by, or was waiting for the presence of our goddess to restore the powers which Winter had benumbed, brought us to Pisa, where, we need not tell our friends, the celebrated Tower has leaned for more than six hundred years and been a source of attraction to thousands visiting the land. Of course we went to its very summit, up the stairs which wind about its eight stories, and there sat down to contemplate the scene. Although our point of observation overhung the base to the extent of fifteen feet, yet we felt no fear, for the centre of gravity lay ten feet within the base, and we looked upon the sun, as it went out of sight, in perfect composure, and rejoiced that its brilliant setting portended a fine day for our ride over the Appenines.

It was even so, the finest of days, and seven o'clock saw us at the depot for the short ride to the Gulf of Spezia, where we took the more desirable carriage, throwing back its top to let us look upon the grand mountain scenery, and drawn by four noble steeds. Over the Appenines! In Italy especially, the bays are beautiful, the lakes are lovely, and the cities are curious; but on the morning of which we write the country was charming and the mountains magnificent. The wand of Spring had produced a magical effect, and a halo of freshness encircled the earth, a golden haze floated in the air. The little village of Spezia looked like an Aladdin's palace on the borders of the bright water, gilded with the lustre of the sun's rays, and it is not strange that the Romans called it the Portus Lunæ (Gate of the Moon); indeed, we fancied we were accompanying the identical Old Man whose features are so often traced by the romantic in the fair orb of Luna, for the route was so enchanting; the modest little marguerites nestled along the roadside and the golden anemones were showered upon us, while little feet kept pace with the rolling wheels and little hands were extended into our very midst, pleading that it was better for us to give than to receive. The peaks appeared in rapid succession, but just as rapidly disappeared, and it was all one beautiful, changing panorama. Our guide did not for one moment desert us, although she was not so profuse in the variety she presented the entire route, and on the neighboring summits we could see that Winter had not yet yielded the sceptre to the queen following so closely upon his footsteps. All along our winding way occasional glimpses of the sparkling sea contrasted beautifully with the bare brown rocks and the sombre evergreens and the purple heather, and our trip across the Appenines, with our number increased by the addition of two to our party, will ever be prominent in our "sunny memories of foreign lands."

The mountains crossed, the sea-shore reached, and then commenced such a roaring, and screeching, and diving into darkness, that we could imagine we were playing hide-and-seek with the imps of the infernal realms. It was, however, only the cars passing in and out from the many tunnels on the road to Genoa.

From the home of Columbus to Milan and Lake Como — the lake so famous, so justly famous ; the lake whose beauties the artist has delineated with the tints of the rainbow and the shades of the sunset, which the poet has portrayed in sweet-sounding rhyme and soft-rolling verse, but whose beauties are best seen from the hand of the Master Artist and in the book of Nature. Our place of sojourn was at Bellaggio, where the two arms come up from Lucca and from Como, unite in one body, and flow on in one round of loveliness.

It was at the broad hour of noon that the Three went forth from the little, close Italian town, leaving behind the workers in olive-wood, and going up higher to sit under the vine and olive, there to feast the body and please the mind, to delight the eye and rejoice the soul. Picnics are always pleasant affairs, and we remember many in the year of wandering and some in the years before we crossed the sea, but none with more pleasure than the one taken on the heights of Bel Monte the first day of April, 1874. The sky was our covering, of a blue so fair and yet so deep that it seemed to reach to the very portal of heaven, and the fleecy clouds, so soft and white, sailed swiftly on toward the haven of rest. The mountains in the dim distance lifted their snowy summits so etherially and so uncertainly that it was impossible to say where earth was finished and heaven begun, and the peaks in the near horizon rolled along like the billows of ocean, bearing upon their breasts the moving shadows of the clouds. The hand of the early springtime was upon everything about us ; tenderest green decked the brown branches, varied with the pink of the prunella and peach, and the shrubs were so delicate that we scarcely knew whether they bore leaves or flowers, while the golden anemones shone in the grass by the side of the meek and modest daisies. On our right and on our left, down through the vines and olives, all this loveliness was repeated over and over again in the waters of the two lakes as they rolled around the green point with its far-seeing palace, and joyfully leaped on to receive together the sunny skies and silvery clouds, the snow-capped mountains and vine-clad hills. Who would not have enjoyed the picnic on Lake Como?

A sail of two and a half hours, a flying trip on the railroad, and we halt at Milan, and at early sunrise visit the Cathedral. "Strange, pure, immaculate mountain of airy unearthly loveliness—the most striking emblem of God's mingled vastness and sweetness that ever it was given to human heart to desire or hands to execute. If there be among the many mansions of our Father above, among the houses not made with hands, aught purer and fairer, it must be the work of those grand spirits who inspired and presided over the erection of this celestial miracle of beauty—thousands of glorified saints standing on a thousand airy points of brilliant whiteness ever solemnly adoring. It had the etherial translucence of wintry frost-work. The beautiful plains of Lombardy lie beneath like a map, and the northern horizon line is glittering with the entire sweep of the Alps like a solemn senate of archangels with diamond mail and glittering crowns. Mount Blanc, Monte Rosa with its countenance of light, the Jungfrau, and all the weird brothers of the Oberland, rise one after another to the delighted gaze and the range of the Tyrol melts far off into the blue of the sky. On another side the Apennines, with their picturesque outlines and cloud-spotted sides, complete the enclosure. All around is the unbroken phalanx of mountains. And this temple, with its thousand saintly statues standing in attitudes of ecstacy and prayer, seems like a worthy altar and shrine for the beautiful plain which the mountains enclose; it seems to give all northern Italy to God.

ILLUSTRATIONS.—1. Tower of Pisa. 2. Leaning Tower of Bologna, (see page 140.) 3. Milan Cathedral. 4. Leonardo da Vinci. 5. Last Supper.

One can fancy there a band of white-robed kings and priests forever ministering in that great temple of which the Alps and the Apennines are the walls and the Cathedral the heart and centre. Never were Nature and Art so majestically married by Religion in so worthy a temple." So says Mrs. Stowe, and we say, of all the beautiful things our eyes looked upon in foreign lands, nothing could surpass the summit of Milan Cathedral.

At Milan, too, is that most beautiful production of the hand of man — the Last Supper — painted on the wall of a room where one would scarce look for aught of this kind. In the refectory of a convent, which has even been used as a stable, is the original of the painting which established the reputation of Leonardo da Vinci. "He was occupied two years in painting this picture. The knowledge of character displayed in the heads of the different Apostles is even more wonderful than the skillful arrangement of the figures and the amazing beauty of the workmanship. The space occupied by the picture is a wall twenty-eight feet in length, the figures being larger than life. Leonardo has contrived to break the formality of the line of heads without any apparent artifice, and without disturbing the general simplicity and order, and has imparted to a solemn scene sufficient movement and variety of action without detracting from its dignity and pathos; he has kept the expression of each head true to its traditional character, without exaggeration, without effort. The intellectual elevation, the fineness of nature, the benign God-like dignity, suffused with the profoundest sorrow in Christ, surpasses all conceived as possible in art."—" Sacred legendary Art."

HOMEWARD BOUND.

Chapter XIX.

MORE than four months before, we entered Italy on Thanksgiving Day, and coming over the peaks where Winter had already spread her white carpet, we left the snowy regions and dwelt in one long, continual springtime. On one of the first days of April we took our places in the cars, with hearts full of thanksgiving that we had wandered in the lands where the pious Æneas, and Romulus and Remus, and scores of others whose names are written in the book of fame, wandered before us. We came *over* the mountains, but we went *under* the mountains — not, however, until we had gone up so high that we greatly feared Spring would retreat and leave us in the icy hands from which we had been striving all these months to escape. We passed through tunnels innumerable, and finally, in the midst of fast-falling snow-flakes, entered that longest one which the world yet knows, and passed over seven and a half miles where the sun never shines — thirty-five minutes under the ground.

In France we saw the light again, and here too the snow was falling upon Mont Cenis; but we steamed on, and one day more brought us to the beautiful city of Paris.

A few hours ride from this justly-famed city, our car —"Pour les Dames"— was entered by four French *dames* of the type we have always imagined those of the terrible days of the French Revolution — of

the days so graphically described in the Tale of Two Cities, when the "Sharp maiden La Guillotine" received so many victories from the hands of the rough French women. These women did not wear the tri-colored cockade, but that which was somewhat akin to it—the high-colored turban; and as Madame Defarge was always knitting during the Reign of Terror, they were busily plying their needles in the bustle and jar of travel; they lost nothing, however, that was passing about them. Two other women were occupying the car, each with a child; first they catechised the little French girl and learned all the circumstances of the past and present, then commenced with the American girl, who scarcely knew how to answer their questions. After they had asked for a song in the English language, it was but meet and proper that they should sing the Marseillaise in the accent and style of the true French citizeness; but at the suggestion they seemed to shrink and not to realize that the watchwords of the French Republic — "Liberté, Egalité, Fraternité" — were the rule and order of the day. After some consultation, however, one of their number sang, in low tones, the grand old air which has so incited "*Aux armes, citoyens.*" So we heard the Marseillaise sung by a French woman in her own *patrie*. Six weeks among the people, whose native tongue takes the traveler throughout Europe, six weeks in their schools and their churches, in their shops and their homes, six weeks with the daily gazette in our hands to inform us of the transactions in the capital city.

One item of news on the first days of May was the following:—"*Les premieres cerises de l'annee vrennint de faire leur apparition a Paris.*" Cherries! ierry is excellent for the teeth in our native land, why not in the land across the Atlantic? Again, "*I mai, grandes eaux a Versailles.*" Preparations were immediately made to attend the grand play of waters at the Palace of Versailles, and on the morning designated we

---

ILLUSTRATIONS.—1. Palace of Versailles, Forest and Fountains.

could not afford the time for the exercise of pedestrianism, so we took a somewhat novel mode of patronizing steam and the iron road. On the top of the cars, where it was somewhat airy, but from which was obtained a magnificent view of the surrounding country, we rode twelve miles to visit Versailles. Versailles! the hunting ground of the Louis, sixty miles in circumference, the home of monarchs for an entire century, the palace where the guards of Marie Antoinette were massacred, and the room where she was sleeping when the mob burst upon her, the Grand and Petit Trianons where the Louis kept their madames in luxury and ease, the most interesting combination of nature and art, the great forest trees varied with statues and fountains. (Oh! who can describe them?) Paris is the capital of France, but it is at Versailles that the Assembly meets in modern days and administers rule to the young republic "*Vive la République!*"

On the 14th of May, 1874, we said our final *adieux au Paris* at the mid-day hour, crossed the Marne (truly meandering) eight times, came in close proximity to the residences of the familiar French writers Bossuet, La Fontaine, and Rousseau, saw the place where Attila was defeated in 431, and after a ride of twenty hours reached the Argentoratum of ancient history — the city which the Romans took from the Celts before the time of Christ — Strasburg, which for the last centuries has been so much in doubt as to whether they should acknowledge Germany the Vaterland, and drink lager beer, singing, "*Fest steht und treu die Wacht die Wacht am Rheim*," or "*Enfants de la Patrie France*," should march to the music of the Marseillaise sipping the sweet wines. The tallest church spire which the world can claim meets the eye of the traveler long before he enters this contested city, and unrolls its beautiful lace work from base to pinnacle. (This spire is 468 feet high, only 24 feet

---

ILLUSTRATIONS.—1. Cathedral and the Storks. 2. Old Palace. 3. Clock. 4. Statue of Guttenberg, Inventor of Printing. 5. Inventor of the Clock. 6. Reformers.

less than the tallest Egyptian pyramid.) It is not strange that some of the random shots from French or German cannon should have disturbed somewhat the well-wrought patterns, but it is much more strange that it should stand a cathedral still in spite of siege with shot and shell. We shall attempt to enlarge upon only one of the many points of this interesting structure — the astronomical clock, the wonder of the world, invented in 1573. At the base of this clock stands a globe representing the motions of our planetary system. The earth moves around the plane of its orbit in 24 hours, Saturn in 30 years, Jupiter in 12, Mars in 2, the Sun, Mercury and Venus in 1, and the Moon in one month. In the middle frame is an artrolabe showing the daily positions of each planet in the signs of the zodiac. There is the skull of a dead man and statues of two boys, one of whom turns the hour-glass when the clock has struck; the other puts forth the rod in his hand at each stroke of the clock. There are statues of Spring, Summer, Autumn and Winter. Youth, Old Age and Death strike the quarters, passing around in procession with measured pace every hour and standing between the quarters with face or back in view, the going and the coming, the past and the future. But at the mid-day hour the room is crowded to witness the procession of the twelve apostles which daily walk around at the very summit, each bowing low as he comes in front of the Saviour to receive his benediction, while the cock claps his wings and crows clearly three times before Peter denies his Lord.

Everywhere a pleasant picture was presented to view of feathered families watching over the city oft-disturbed, as the goose saved the Roman capital from the invasion of savage hordes, only that was in the night time, and it is under the eye of bright old Sol that the storks take their stand as sentinels of Strasburg. May their nests be undisturbed and their families unbroken by the shrill war trumpet and the leaden bullet of death, but may the spirit of Gutenburg hover over the scene and carry forward the invention he gave to the world — printing.

One mile away Father Rhine takes his waters joyfully on toward the castles and invites us again to seek what before became to us "*Chateaux en Espagne,*" (castles in the air.) But we turn a deaf ear for we have heard of Heidelberg Castle, (which, "next to the Alhambra of Grenada, is the most magnificent ruin of the middle ages,") and Heidelberg University, and we spend a Sabbath on the banks of the Neckar, in the region so replete with incidents of the Reformation, we enter that famous church where Jerome of Prague, the friend of Huss, fastened his theses; and a more wonderful church still which accommodates Catholics and Protestants under one and the same roof, the Church of the Holy Ghost, where we read on the walls "*Eine feste Burg ist unser Gott,*" and just before the door we saw the faces of the well-known reformers, Luther, Huss, Jerome of Prague, etc. Above the picturesque Neckar to the castle, around Heidelberg Tun, the largest cask in the world, capable of containing 800 hogsheads but which was never filled but once, and we came back to rest in our room at the hotel, when a glance from the window showed an exhibition so truly unique that we were anxious to see it — a dog dance. In a rumbling cart rode eight or ten varieties of the canine race, from the wee poodle to the grim old mastiff, all sitting like majors on the seats prepared for them; and when they were placed upon the ground and their captain, with two legs instead of four, made music and called off for them to dance, they did better than some we have seen in parlors, and we are sure that the German dogs are accomplished in this line at least.

Through Worms, where we had a little quarrel with the conductor, just to remember the city where Luther was summoned to appear before the Diet, (not where he dieted on worms, as a certain little girl understood it,) we arrive at Mayence, where we take a rapid retrospect of the glimpses we have had of the river on whose banks we stand, ready to try the realities of a sail on the Rhine. No one can say that the Three

---

ILLUSTRATION.—Cathedral of Strasburg.

did not stand at its very source when they walked in the cloud over the Pass of St. Gothard, where the cold waters rolled from their icy bed and bathed their feet as they wandered almost lost in the mist and fog; at Schaffhausen its waters dashed over the rocks, and we sailed with them, all befogged, on to Lake Constance, not a castle taking form to our searching eyes; but at a time when March winds and April showers and May flowers all formed part of a glorious Spring day, we were launched upon the waters which romance and reality have alike invested with interest, and sailed along the banks where fable and fact have striven to outdo each other in incident and act.

Bulwer says:—" What the Tiber is to the classic, the Rhine is to the chivalric age. The steep rock and the gray, dismantled tower, the massive and rude picturesque of the feudal days, constitute the great feature of the scene; you might almost fancy, as you are sailing along, that you are gliding back down the river of Time, the monuments of the pomp and power of old rising, one after another, upon its shores."

It was a suitable starting-place, where the ruins of the ramparts of Drusus Germanicus and remnants of the fortifications of Augustus Cæsar mingled with the modern martial appearance of this strong German fortress; and with the "Legends" in our hands and the castellated banks before our eyes, we were at a loss as to whether we were creatures of to-day or roaming spirits of other days. Oh, what castles we saw and what castles we built that day on the Rhine!—castles among the rivers and castles among the clouds, castles that time has crumbled and left more beautiful as the centuries rolled by, and castles that the winds of heaven have scattered and gathered together—the *were* and the *to be;* but "King Rhine" ruled over them all, and we were his most devoted subjects. That these beauties might linger and not vanish like castles in the air, we landed at fair Bingen, so touchingly bewailed by "a soldier of the legion" who "lay dying in Algiers," and we wandered for hours in the Drusus castle, where the Cæsars looked down from the green walls upon us, and we looked down into the dungeons where kings have been captives; also by the Mouse Tower, rising from a picturesque island, where the mice followed Bishop Hatto and devoured his body, which incident Southey has versified as a warning to those who are unkind to the poor. We viewed the Ehrenfels, hanging upon the rock on the opposite bank, and the Niederwald, so high that eagles and robbers alone would make it a home, and we slept in their shadow, the moon adding her soft tale to the many already told.

Another day was filled with visions fair — the peaks where firm and true stands the Watch on the Rhine, and where the beautiful syren sings her sweet song and lures the unwary to destruction.

"High, and dark, and massive, swell the towers and rock of Ehrenbreitstein, a type of that great chivalric spirit — the honor that the rock arrogates for its name, which demands so many sacrifices of blood and tears, but which ever creates in the restless heart of man a far deeper interest than the more peaceful scenes of life by which it is contrasted." Ehrenbreitstein commands the Rhine and the Moselle, and just opposite, at Coblentz, ("Confluentia,") is the church where the grandsons of Charlemagne met to divide the countries of Germany, France and Italy. We went back to the time, too, when Cæsar crossed the Rhine, seventeen centuries ago. Back amidst the sloping mountains the famous battle between paganism and Christianity was fought and the cross appeared to Constantine, and wars innumerable have been carried on upon these banks. Lastly the Siebengebirge (Seven Mountains) rose in grandeur and bade us adieu as we sailed under

"The castled crag of Drachenfels."

ILLUSTRATIONS.—1. Bingen with Ehrenbreitstein on the left and Rheinstein on the right. 2. Van Dyck and Rubens. 3. Cathedral at Cologne. 4. Cathedral at Aix-la-Chapelle where Charlemagne is buried. 5. Royal Family of England. 6. Kenilworth Castle in the 16th century and in the 19th.

The glories of the Rhine are passed, and we marvel and dream till we reach Cologne. Cologne! City best known to the world in general by the fragrant liquid, *eau de Cologne*, which constitutes so important an item in the boudoir of the beau and belle, (much of which, however, never comes further than from the walls of their own apothecary shop,) —city which owes its origin to Marcus Agrippa, the Roman who first placed a camp on one of the surrounding hills, and its name to Agrippina, the mother of the infamous Nero, who was born in the camp of her father, Germanicus, and the place was called Colonia Agrippina, whence Cologne. This city appropriates its part of the legends of the Rhine, as the Church of St. Ursula with its bones of eleven thousand virgins murdered by Attila, and the Cathedral with its monument to the three Magi who came from the East to worship Christ, would show. Here is one of the masterpieces of Rubens, the Crucifixion of the Apostle with his head downwards, in the church where is still shown the font in which he was baptized.

Now farewell to the waters of the Rhine, for we go by rail to Aix-la-Chapelle, so closely connected with the name of Charlemagne. The cathedral here was commenced in 796, under Charlemagne, who lies in the centre of the octagon beneath the dome, so that the sun at mid-day falls directly upon his tomb. We were told that in the year 1000 his grave was opened and the chair in which he was buried sitting now stands in the Town Hall with other relics and mementoes of the great Charles. Here ended the career of one who swayed gracefully the rod of empire, and lay down in the midst of the monuments he had reared to sleep the last long sleep that knows no waking. From Rome to Aix-la-Chapelle his name and his statues are frequently met, and here we leave him in his last home. Truly every place, as well as person, has its own peculiarities, and the one we observed in the German Aachen (Aix) was that all marriage ceremonies are performed in the Rathhaus or Town

Hall, and on the occasion of our visit to that locality nine waiting couples were watching the minute-hand to see when the hour of twelve would arrive!

At Brussels, the Belgian capital, begin the beautiful carvings in wood which adorn the cathedrals. Godfrey of Bouillon, celebrated chief of the First Crusade, rides as life-like in the Royal Square as if leading his followers in the glorious cause; and Egmont and Horn stand in front of the house where they spent the night before their execution.

Ten miles from Brussels is the field of Waterloo, where in four days of the year 1815 more than one hundred thousand men gave their lives to decide the fate of Europe and send Napoleon the Great to the island of St. Helena.

It is enough to say of Antwerp that it is the commercial capital of Belgium, on the Scheldt, and the birthplace of Rubens and Van Dyck. The Cathedral of Notre Dame contains the Elevation to and the Descent from the Cross, beside many other of the finest paintings of Rubens. In the Church of St. James is his Holy Family, in which he copied the members of his family, and here too is his own tomb. Rubens and Van Dyck are highly honored in their native city, and their statues are prominent in the most public place. A curious lesson is taught by one of the paintings. In the Museum at Antwerp, the "Fallen Angels" was the production of a leading artist, who had decided that none but an artist should claim his daughter's hand. Unfortunately she was loved and sought by one who was only a blacksmith, and he learned the irrevocable decision of the father of the young lady. Nothing daunted, however, he abandoned his original trade and took up the brush. After months of indefatigable study, he visited the artist's studio, and seeing this painting just completed, he represented an enormous bee crawling on the thigh of one of the angels, so perfect that one shudders and almost feels the sting, and so perfect that Flors received Matsys as his son-in-law. We need not always keep the same position in life, if we have only energy and perseverance enough to exercise the talents given unto us.

At Ghent the two went in haste to the cathedral to see the finest carving in wood the world affords. The tree of life supports the pulpit, and Time, a venerable old man, sits at the foot, attempting to raise a veil and look upon Truth, who approaches with a book in which are the words, "Arise, thou that sleepest, and Christ shall give thee light." We were sufficiently rewarded for our walk and hurry, and again were in the cars for Mechlin and Bruges.

One more night on the continent, beneath the Belfry of Bruges, and what beautiful chimes rang the night away! Every quarter of an hour a sweet serenade for the wandering Three United States Girls, and the chimes of memory often waft us back and we hear them again, the Chimes of Bruges.

From Ostend to Dover across the channel, and we are in the land where our native tongue is spoken, just one year older than the day we sailed from New York harbor. On the anniversary of that day we sit within the walls of Westminster Abbey, that antique pile where the suns of empire rise and set, listening to the soft chanting of the choir and the solemn notes of the organ as the sun sends its last brilliant ray in upon the tombs of the great and the noble, and lights up the pillars and the carving, the oak and the marble of this royal burial-place in a grand and striking manner. While we listen and gaze a noble array of churches rises before our mind's eye. Far back on Roman soil rises that mother of Catholic churches, St. Peter's, the largest in Europe and the world, (with one exception). Everywhere in this most noble structure appear the marks of the master-painter and sculptor Raphael and Michael Angelo, and as their genius towered above that of all other men so the labor of their hands rises high over all. Three hundred other churches cluster about the largest one and render Rome a prominent place although so far away. Next rises that dome which served as a model for St. Peter's and which exceeds it in size. The Duomo of Florence, the dome which admits the light of heaven upon the tombs of its architects, surrounding them with a bright halo as fame illuminates the names of Giotto and Brunelleschi. There we see the picturesque front where stand the horses so well known, the horses of St. Mark, and we remember well how the thousand years have left the marks of time and age on the dark walls within, while the external appearance is that of lightness and grace and beauty. The doves play around her head and the gondolas ply at her feet and Venice may well be proud of St. Mark. Miles away rises the most beautiful cathedral of Milan, its thousand marble pinnacles towering heavenward like the peaks of the Alps in the far distance. Notre Dame lifts her square towers from the island in the Seine and shows the spot where kings and emperors have had their day, but where no crowned head now rules. Republic of France! Near the banks of the Rhine the spire of Strasburg shows its lace-work summit — the tallest of spires over that most wonderful clock which marks the passage of time in many curious ways. Then Cologne lifts its unfinished dome over the city where Rubens was born, and over (they say) the tombs of the three wise men who came from the far east to worship Christ. We recognize from Aix-la-Chapelle the octagonal spire which admits the rays of the sun upon the tomb of Charlemagne in the city which gave him birth and which took its name from the same interesting work commenced by him in the eighth century. Brussels, Antwerp, Ghent, and Bruges, all mark this picture painted from memory with their cathedrals most beautifully ornamented with carvings in wood and containing the most precious works of Rubens and Van Dyck. From all these churches we seem to hear one continual chant and to see one round of service performed by priests and people in a foreign tongue, and we come back to the land of our fore-

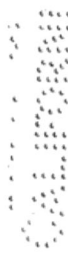

HOUSE IN WHICH SHAKESPEARE WAS BORN

fathers to the language of our native land, and into the presence of the illustrious dead, where one at least has found rest from his wanderings since we worshipped before in Westminster Abbey— Dr. Livingstone, borne by savages from a savage land, to sleep at home in the midst of his friends. Blessed rest! Sweet sleep!

Nine days in London, as busy as three millions can make it, and we steam away one hundred miles to Stratford-upon-Avon,

"Where his first infant lays sweet Shakspeare sung,
Where the last accents faltered on his tongue,"

and here, in the spot to which the genius of one man has given immortality, we linger a day, in the rooms of his birth-place, crossing the fields to Anne Hathaway's cottage, and looking upon his bust above the slab which covers the ashes of one of whom the world has never known the like. Westminster covets his precious dust, and it is said that once it was nearly removed there; but the curse called down upon those attempting his disinterment, by the pen of the great poet himself, withheld them from accomplishing their designs.

True descendants of our English mothers, two of us went over the English highways, between the sweet hedges of English hawthorn, counting the minutes between the mile-stones till eight were passed in the space of two hours. After a night at Leamington, a walk of five miles brought us to Kenilworth, of which Scott has written:—"Of this lordly palace, where princes feasted and heroes fought, now in the bloody earnest of storm and siege, and now in the games of chivalry, where beauty dealt the prize which valor won, all is now desolate. The bed of the lake is a rushy swamp, and the massy ruins of the castle only serve to show what their splendor once was."

To Chester and Liverpool, and then to Glasgow, ready to take the Anchor Line across the sea, and

---

ILLUSTRATIONS,—1. Home of Shakspeare at Stratford-on-Avon. 2. Monument of Shakspeare 3. Tomb of Bunyan in Bunhill Fields, London.

> The shades of night were falling fast,
> As forth from Glasgow's shores we passed,
> In a ship that bore on the afterpart
> A name that will live in every heart—
> The *California*.
>
> The time flew by on golden wing;
> We had sailed in tears, we were landing in song;
> Days were never so joyous or hours so short
> As those that vanished between us and port,
> On the *California*.

Ten days we were rocked on old Ocean's bosom, ten days we sailed under a sunny sky, and out on the face of the broad deep we celebrated the ninety-eighth birthday of our glorious Union. We landed in safety on the sixth of July, and felt that no one could more proudly cry the watchwords they had in the beginning adopted than the

INDEPENDENT DAUGHTERS OF UNCLE SAM.

www.ingramcontent.com/pod-product-compliance
Lightning Source LLC
Chambersburg PA
CBHW031251250426
43672CB00029BA/2089